YOUR MARRIAGE CAN SURVIVE A NEWBORN

GLENN & NATALIE WILLIAMS

BROADMAN
& HOLMAN
PUBLISHERS

NASHVILLE, TENNESSEE

© 2005 by Glenn Allan Williams
All rights reserved.
Printed in the United States of America

13-digit ISBN: 978-0-8054-4060-7
10-digit ISBN: 0-8054-4060-7

Published by Broadman & Holman Publishers,
Nashville, Tennessee

Dewey Decimal Classification: 306.8
Subject Heading: MARRIAGE \ PARENT AND CHILD

First published in Australia in 2004 as *Your Relationship Can Survive a Newborn,* a Focus on the Family book published by Focus on the Family International. © Baby Blues Partnership. Reprinted with special permission of King Features Syndicate

All Scripture quotations, unless otherwise indicated, are taken from the Holman Christian Standard Bible © 1999, 2000, 2002, 2003 by Holman Bible Publishers, Nashville, Tennessee; all rights reserved. Verses marked NIV are from the Holy Bible, New International Version ®, NIV®, © 1973, 1978, 1984 by International Bible Society; used by permission of Zondervan Publishing House; all rights reserved.

1 2 3 4 5 6 7 8 9 10 09 08 07 06 05

Dedicated to:

Our Parents

Colin and Betty Bunnett

Max Williams

Our Children

Benjamin

Ryan

Chloe

In Loving Memory of

Irene Williams

Contents

Acknowledgments

This book was birthed out of a desire to encourage parents of newborns and to help them know they are not alone in their journey. Over time as we found the courage to be honest about the challenges our relationship faced when a newborn arrived home, many of our friends encouraged and helped us in the writing process.

We are grateful for the many stories others shared with us and the creative and practical ideas they passed on to us so we could in turn pass them on to you.

There really are so many people we could thank for different reasons. Friends who encouraged us to persevere when we felt like giving up, and others who assured us that this was a book every parent of a newborn needs.

We particularly want to single out our deep appreciation for Marianne Hering as our editor. She drew out stories we had forgotten and helped us to describe our experiences in such a way that people would want to keep on reading. Marianne's sensitivity and patience were important factors in getting us to finish writing this book.

We also want to express our gratitude to other members of the editorial team—Bruce Peppin and Sandy Bové, and the wonderful support provided by Focus on the Family's International department.

Finally, we want to thank Win Morgan—a colleague, a writer, and a longtime friend—who inspired us to write down our thoughts and feelings so that others might be encouraged. Thank you!

CHAPTER 1

The Baby Bomb

Natalie and I thought we'd heard all the horror stories about giving birth and the sleepless nights that were to follow. We had friends who relished in telling us what it was really like—one friend who hated the sight of blood and fainted early in the delivery process only to be revived just as his wife was about to give birth. (We're not sure he was ever forgiven and eighteen years later is still trying to make amends.) Another friend described how he felt about the sleepless nights that followed the birth of his daughter by referring to them as "The Never-Ending Story."

But after listening for hours to our friends fondly recall and sometimes embellish their birthing stories, we never heard them describe how hard the first few weeks would be on our relationship. It was only when we began to talk to our friends and family about how frustrated we felt that they would open up and share how caring for a newborn was one of the most difficult times in their relationship, too.

All parents have a unique story to tell about the time leading up to the birth of their child. After interviewing dozens of parents, we learned that no matter how excited and nervous they may have been about having a baby, those first few minutes, weeks, and months after their baby's birth were greatly affected by each parent's differing personality, family upbringing, and experience during the pregnancy. These critical factors influenced our experience in ways we had not imagined. The area in which we experienced the most surprising change, however, was our relationship.

> Tension crept into our relationship after the birth of our first son because our lives had become absorbed and preoccupied with getting things ready for him.

Tension crept into our relationship after the birth of our first son because our lives had become absorbed and preoccupied with getting things ready for him. We suddenly noticed a radical shift in our focus from our needs to the baby's needs. Of course our needs had not vanished and, in fact, had become even greater under this new stress, but it seemed that they always were drowned out by our son's extremely vocal demands.

As exciting as the experience of having a baby can be, we began to understand that there was also a sense of loss. For about seven years we only had to think of each other's needs. It was relatively easy fitting in with each other and accommodating each other's needs, desires, and goals. Those days were gone. We were now confronted with the reality that we had to fit someone else into our lives and attend to a new set of needs. That would mean reprioritizing our own needs, perhaps even to the exclusion of them.

Some people take this fear of a changed relationship to an extreme. We have a friend whose fiancé wanted her to forgo having children if they were to get married because he was afraid it would destroy their relationship as it had his own parents. A December 2003 report by Relationships Australia indicated that an increasing number of couples were more interested in friendship and intimacy than in having children. And there is no doubt that children will impact a couple's relationship—but it doesn't have to be bad. Facing the struggles of parenting together can often result in a better, stronger, more mature relationship.

Our reactions, our expectations, and how well we adapt to these changes will influence how positive or negative these impacts will be.

It is easy to find books on what to expect in the baby's development over the first six weeks to a year, but Natalie and I found little available on how to help our relationship survive this incredibly stressful time—the baby-bomb period.

In recognition of this we wrote this book to provide you with some constructive and positive tips to encourage you during what some parents describe as one of the most challenging and yet exciting times in their relationship. We found that even with our third child, we still had to learn and make adjustments in our relationship.

By sharing about our experiences we're hoping that you might find some small snippets of hope from our journals and read something to keep you sane.

Remember: This book is not about parenting a newborn. It's about helping your relationship with your spouse grow and survive. Ultimately, these pages are to encourage you. We hope that you'll appreciate the thoughts and ideas in them, which have been gleaned from our own life and from many hours of talking to other parents. What follows is part of our story—a description of our feelings, frustrations, and minor victories as we struggled to maintain a healthy relationship after the birth of our son. We share these memories in hope that your journey through parenthood may be a little easier.

The Conception

The birth of our first child was nothing like Glenn and I (Natalie) expected. We had been trying to have children for a year and a half, and the months leading up to the news that I was pregnant had been an emotional roller coaster. Each month we looked forward to learning if we were about to become parents. After several disappointments, I began to wonder if something was wrong with me physically and if I would ever be able to conceive a child.

So you can imagine how excited and nervous I was when the pregnancy test showed positive—two pink lines appeared.

Having already gone through a number of these tests in previous months, when the second pink line gradually appeared, I was over the moon. I checked those little pink lines at least a dozen times to make sure I wasn't hallucinating, and then asked Glenn to check it almost as many times. Glenn still remembers how excited I was, as it was about five o'clock in the morning (and he is not renowned for being a morning person). He was still half-asleep when I ran into the room and jumped up and down on the bed. Needless to say, he jolted awake and shared in my excitement.

We waited about fourteen weeks before we gave the news to both sets of prospective grandparents. They couldn't believe how long we had waited before telling them. We made a decision to wait until we knew that everything was OK. We knew that our parents would be excited—particularly my parents, because this would be their first grandchild. I didn't want to disappoint my parents if I miscarried. I knew that there was a higher risk of miscarriage in the first three months, and so it was important to me to get through that period.

Naturally they all were excited. My mother was a first-time grandmother and wanted to celebrate by going shopping for baby clothes. Even though Glenn's parents already had five grandchildren, they were still excited and his mom especially was looking forward to enjoying our first baby by going shopping and babysitting with my mom.

Like every other expectant mother, I experienced the normal concerns regarding the changes to my body, and committed to doing everything I possibly could to make sure that I delivered a healthy baby. My two biggest fears were that I might miscarry or that our baby would not be born healthy. It seemed that the closer the pregnancy moved toward the delivery date, the more anxious I became about my baby's health.

Everything throughout the pregnancy went along smoothly. While I had my fears that something could still go wrong, my mind often jumped to thinking about what my life would be like after the birth.

I had enjoyed a challenging career as an occupational therapist for nine years and managing other therapists in the delivery of care to patients. But I still wondered how I would perform as a mother responding to the needs of my baby. I also like to be in control. I make lists and plan my days. Being highly structured helps me to accomplish all the things I want to get done. Would I be able to manage a baby who would probably resist structure?

While I didn't care to admit it, I was also concerned about what others would think if we didn't adapt to parenthood. After all, I was an occupational therapist and Glenn was a psychologist. We had all the right credentials and were expected to do well.

I was anticipating the changes of becoming a parent and looked forward to the growth process. I read a plethora of books about what to expect as my child developed. What I wasn't as prepared for were the changes in my relationship with Glenn. Even after being married for six years before having a baby, I wasn't expecting the challenges I would face as his parenting-partner.

The Bomb Detonates

I (Glenn) sensed a tremendous responsibility for our unborn child and knew that I had many things still to learn about caring for him. Although we heard friends talk about how hard it was getting up in the middle of the night, what it was like to function during the day with little sleep, and how hard it would be trying to settle a crying baby, at the time it wasn't something I could relate to. Only later did it begin to make sense.

Thinking about becoming a parent also invoked an amazing array of emotions, thoughts, expectations, and assumptions that were difficult to grapple with. I realized that my own experience of being parented influenced the type of parent I wanted to be. I would ask Natalie questions like "What are the things you like about your parents?" "How do you want to be different?" and "What did you like the most about how your parents related to each other and supported each other?" Although we had previously discussed these things superficially, I knew I would soon be faced with having to make decisions about them. Would I be ready?

Even after being married for six years before having a baby, I wasn't expecting the challenges I would face as his parenting-partner.

Then after all those months of waiting, it finally happened: Our son was born. What an exhilarating moment! I'm still not sure who was relieved the most, Natalie or I. I felt so helpless watching and encouraging her during the labor experience, and being able to do nothing more, though I am pretty sure I wouldn't have wanted to change places!

In that short journey through the birth canal, my son experienced vast changes. He would now need to breathe on his own, regulate his own body temperature, learn how to drink from his mother's breast, and discover the ability to stretch his arms and legs out uninhibited. In the minutes and hours after the delivery, our heads were spinning, and our world seemed a blur. From listening to stories our friends shared and reading books leading up to the birth of our son, we had expected these changes. What we found, however, was that we weren't ready for how his arrival would change our relationship almost as radically. The baby bomb had dropped!

CHAPTER 2

What Have We Done?

Many parents describe the birth of their child as a miracle and a significant spiritual moment in their lives. Certainly that was how Natalie and I felt when Ben was born. Although this miracle is sparked from an intimate experience between two people, the experience of creating a new life transcends humanness—it is the handiwork of something divine. As parents, you have become a link in an amazing physiological and biological chain that is too wonderful to have ever been created by chance.

Whether the birth of your child was a profound spiritual moment or not, very soon you discover that you're praying to make it through the day. Emotionally and physically you are drained. Caring for a newborn demands every ounce of energy you can muster—even more than you think you are capable of.

We found ourselves floundering with being parents from the minute Ben was born. Here's how I, Glenn, felt:

I was in a daze when the obstetrician asked if I would like to cut my son's umbilical cord. As I was handed the appropriate instrument, I was truly afraid that I might hurt my son, until I was told that he wouldn't feel a thing. Was I supposed to know that? Thankfully, the obstetrician guided my hand very carefully, and the deed was done within seconds.

> As parents, you have become a link in an amazing physiological and biological chain that is too wonderful to have ever been created by chance.

With the formalities out of the way, our baby was passed around, hugged, wrapped up, and then unwrapped for a series of checks.

Any abstract fears we had about our son's health were realized concretely in the next few minutes. Doctors discovered that Ben had fluid on the lung that made it difficult for him to breathe. While we both found this quite disturbing, Natalie found it particularly difficult, as she barely had an opportunity to hold her newborn child before he was taken away.

Thankfully, Ben's problem cleared up in a few days, but at that moment I felt helpless and out of control. That was the first shock I had as a father. I had planned and prepared so much in advance for this moment, but in reality I had no true power over the situation at all.

After a few minutes, which seemed like hours, a nurse gave Ben back to Natalie and me. Although we were exhausted by the huge buildup, anxieties about the unknown, and sheer tiredness from pushing (and coaching), we found that the adrenaline kept our eyes open and bodies on remote control. Eventually the nurses and family members left, and we were finally alone.

Here we were, holding a child that came with no instruction manual, no on-and-off switch, and no warranty. His fingers were so tiny and his skin so translucent that he looked like a doll. It struck me that Natalie and I were the sole hope of survival for this delicate creature. The enormity of the responsibilities of parenthood filled my heart with joy—and panic. I wasn't sure if we were up to the task. I found myself looking at this vulnerable creature and asking, "What have we done?"

The Challenge Begins

Glenn and I somehow made it through the first few days, the stress, exhaustion, and frustration of parenthood taking its toll. Our friends and family told of their parenting experiences while visiting us in the hospital, and also at our home afterward when they would drop in for a quick coffee to ogle Ben and check on how we were doing. Some of my friends clearly remembered how challenging caring for a newborn was for them, while others had forgotten. One of my friends found newborn babies no trouble at all. Her experience was that a baby wakes for feeding every three hours and then goes back to sleep. My friends' success stories made me feel as though I was abnormal or that Glenn and I must be doing something wrong.

Sometimes when I was tired or frustrated because Ben wouldn't settle down, I thought, *Are we bad parents? Do other people function with broken sleep throughout the night and respond eagerly every time to a baby that seemingly needed to be fed milk on a drip?*

Yes, both Glenn and I were very happy to be parents. We would have thrown ourselves in front of a train to save Ben, but we didn't yet know what Ben would do to our relationship.

Looking back, I can see that circumstances were stacked against us. Not every couple has the luxury of taking a week or two off work to adjust to parenthood. That's how it was for us. Glenn was constantly in touch with the office due to the national launch of a program his organization had created. This meant that he had to share his deteriorating energy with competing priorities. The ironic thing about this was that the program was an educational program designed to help parents. Certainly, balancing work and family responsibilities was one of those challenging areas that would last well beyond the first few months of parenthood.

There's Nothing Convenient about a Baby

We've heard plenty of reasons for waiting to have children: "We want to enjoy life together for awhile because we know a baby will mean we can't do some of the things we enjoy doing." "We're hoping to put as much money into our mortgage as possible so we can afford to start a family." "I want to work hard to further my career while I can." "If I undertake postgraduate studies now it will be easier for me to resume my career after having a baby." "I want to lose weight first." While it makes good sense to plan when to have a baby so you can organize your priorities, work out a budget, get the house ready, and prepare yourself emotionally, hear this—babies have absolutely nothing to do with convenience!

Even if you've accomplished everything you wanted to before having a baby, your life and your relationship with your spouse are about to radically change shape. Some might call it being naive, but we honestly thought that our baby would comfortably slot into our life with relatively minor adjustments. How wrong we were! The rest of our world didn't stop just because a baby arrived on the scene. Ben had no way of telling when we were experiencing difficulties in managing a demanding work schedule, becoming increasingly frustrated because we couldn't get enough sleep, or missing out on time alone with each other. We discovered that even if you have a baby at home, life keeps moving at the same pace, still slaps you in the face with crises, and is as unpredictable as ever.

Life can be rosy when a newborn arrives. There are lots of warm, special moments like cradling a sleeping child, smelling your baby's skin for the first time, and enjoying the wonder of just being a parent of a newly created human being with your DNA. Wow! But then there are still the thorns, the normal responsibilities you had in your life before you became a parent. You can't throw them out with the dirty diapers.

We had all the same duties, obligations, relationships, and personality traits we had before we had our first child. We just had to learn to manage them all with a dwindling supply of time and energy. This resulted in some tension in our relationship because we didn't have the same resources to support each other that we had before Ben came along.

Our First Crisis

Here's how Natalie describes our first crisis as parents:

Ben's birth coincided with Glenn's mother being critically ill in the hospital. She was undergoing chemotherapy and radiation treatments to eradicate an aggressive cancer in her body. Two tiny tumors in her brain, a growth in one of her lungs, and a growth at the base of the spine were eating her life away. This came as a severe shock to Glenn and his family. We feared that Glenn's mother would not survive to see our first child. This upset Glenn terribly, so much so that we discussed the option of inducing the birth in order to create time for her to hold her grandson.

After taking advice from the doctors, however, we chose not to go that route, and thankfully Glenn's mother survived long enough to meet Ben. Although Glenn told me that I did a great job supporting him during his grieving periods, I often felt as though I had nothing left in my emotional tank to fuel him through this crisis. After Ben's birth, Glenn would come home exhausted and emotionally drained from visiting his mother in the hospital, and all I did was hand Ben over to him so I could go to bed. It wasn't because I didn't care about or love Glenn any less. But the reality was if I was going to get through the next day, I needed to sleep. It may sound a little selfish and overly practical, but as Ben's main caretaker I had to make sure I got some sleep or it would hurt all of us. Glenn certainly didn't get the support and help I would have liked to give him, but I now had two people I loved needing my attention, and the baby, by virtue of his pure helplessness, came first.

Hellos and Good-byes

Here are Glenn's memories:

On the one hand I was overjoyed at the prospect of becoming a dad, but on the other hand, I was painfully and slowly accepting that I was about to lose one of the most significant people in my life, my mother. At times I felt overwhelmed by how incredibly unfair her illness was. My mother was only fifty-nine years old, and up until her surgery, she had been bubbling with life and passion. This was not supposed to happen. Not to her, and not to me at such a significant milestone in my life.

I had this huge emotional pendulum inside of me swinging from one extreme to the other. My moods and emotions fluctuated from feelings of pride, excitement, and nervous anticipation to anger, helplessness, and overwhelming grief knowing that Mom was not going to be around to enjoy my son, and I was not going to have the satisfaction of watching them in each other's company. I had conflicting responsibilities and desires pulling me apart. I had no control over what was happening. Sometimes I felt guilty because I didn't have the energy to support Natalie by reassuring her during those anxious days leading up to Ben's birth. I also felt guilty because I wasn't able to be there for Dad and Mom at a time when family was so important.

After Ben was born I struggled with guilt in a different way. My mother was dying, and here I was enjoying my newborn son. Some of my friends tried to encourage me to view the situation as being "the circle of life," and wasn't it nice that God had blessed me by giving me something positive—the baby—to focus on while my mother was dying. While there was some truth in this, it wasn't much consolation. As far as I was concerned, I didn't want to be dealing with death at all, especially at a time when I should have been celebrating the miracle of life.

Although exhausted the morning after Ben was born, I left Natalie at the hospital to get a roll of film developed so I could take some photos with me when I visited Mom at another hospital. I received the shock of my life when I entered her room. I could barely recognize my own mother because her face was swollen and red; it looked as if it had been severely burned. Since my last visit only two days earlier, Mom had developed an allergic reaction to the cancer-fighting chemicals pumping through her body.

I tried hard to be strong for her, but I could not prevent myself from breaking down. Mom, as usual, was the strong one and overcame her pain to share my excitement when I showed her the photos of Ben. She was so proud. Always the optimist, she said that she would see Ben soon. And she did—in fact, she lived for three months after Ben's birth.

In spite of the pain, the guilt, and the fluctuating emotions, I was so grateful to have Ben. In many ways, he helped me through some of those days when the thought of losing Mom was too much to carry. It was so comforting being able to cradle him and have him snuggle up under my chin. He helped me focus on the blessing of life that was so easy to take for granted.

I discovered firsthand that babies aren't programmed to appear at the most convenient times in our lives. I did not want to juggle the demands of a newborn while coming to terms with my mother's deteriorating health and impending death. Life goes on, however, and things happen for which you can't always be prepared. I was conscious that this was not a great start for us as prospective parents, knowing that we were both physically and emotionally tired and already feeling a little anxious about how we would cope with the changes a baby brings. It's no wonder we would say more than once in the weeks ahead, "What have we done?"

We've Done Well

Even though Ben cried, woke us up from our sleep, and dirtied his diapers at the most inconvenient times, he was part of us. We loved his features: his dimple, his tiny ears, his nose, and those beautiful long eyelashes. We loved hugging him and rocking him to sleep gently in our arms.

We cannot describe for you how we felt when we watched him sleep (aside from the overwhelming relief). It was almost as if he had an angelic quality when he slept.

Our lives have been well and truly changed, and there were times when we wondered if our relationship would survive. Over time, things did get better, and we slowly adjusted our world to include the third member of our family.

There were still quite a few times when we asked ourselves, "What have we done?" But then there were also other unforgettable moments of wonder we have come to treasure that reassure us we have done a wonderful thing indeed.

Quick Tips

- Don't compare your experience with others. Many "successful" parents of newborns are those with very poor memories or were just plain ol' lucky.
- The changes and adaptations you'll make with a newborn are a training period for your relationship. By working through these difficult months, you'll develop the skills re-

quired for parenting and maintaining a great relationship with your spouse. View this as your relationship boot camp. It's tough, but you'll come out stronger.

- Remember, your husband or wife still cares about you, even though he or she may be too busy to show it in the same ways as before.

"A house is built by wisdom,
and it is established by understanding;
by knowledge the rooms are filled
with every precious and beautiful treasure."[1]

CHAPTER 3

Great Expectations

One morning after Glenn said good-bye and left for work, I sat at the kitchen table thinking: *I should be the one going out to work and Glenn should stay home because he is so much better at taking care of Ben than I am.* On the outside I probably looked as though I was totally in control. Showered, dressed, ready to tackle the day. But on the inside I felt anxious and inadequate because I didn't have Glenn around to help me.

Some days Glenn would come home from work to find the house a wreck. I'm sure there must have been times when he wondered how on earth a mother and her infant son could make such a mess—the dishes sitting in the sink, breakfast and lunch plates still on the table, and the bed unmade. Ben wasn't sleeping well, and so when he did take a nap, instead of cleaning up the house I enjoyed some peace and quiet.

This created a little tension in our relationship. Glenn doesn't like sitting down to dinner when there's dirty laundry heaped on the floor or bills and dirty dishes stacked up on the table. After coming home from work he would rather whiz around and do a superficial cleaning before eating. The problem with that was I wanted him to take Ben so I could get dinner ready, not clean the house. I didn't feel like I was being a good mother, a good wife, or a good homemaker.

Not only did I feel inadequate in my new role, but my whole world had radically changed and become so much smaller. I had left a place of employment where I completed projects and had a sense of accomplishment when a patient improved. At home, I could no longer measure success and therefore assumed I was unsuccessful.

The hardest part of my transition to motherhood was that I couldn't clock out when I needed to. I never felt that my day was finished and I could relax and take some time for myself. With the baby, I couldn't look back on my day with a sense of accomplishment over what I had achieved, and I felt that whatever I was supposed to be doing wasn't being done very well. This created a cycle so that it became extremely hard to relax during the day. Not only had my home become my workplace, but the work was never done.

Glenn Had It All

To an extent I began to resent or begrudge Glenn's life. To my way of thinking, he had it all. He would go off to enjoy work and social interaction with his colleagues, and then come home and enjoy the baby. He had a life. I was stuck home with the baby. No longer did I go off to work and enjoy time with my colleagues or come home from work with a sense of fulfillment and accomplishment. My life was now my baby's world.

While I was nearing my maternity leave, I often thought about how nice it would be to stay at home and take things at a more leisurely pace while having a break from full-time work. The concerns I expressed to Glenn were whether I would have enough to do to occupy my time, and that perhaps a baby wouldn't fill up my day and be challenging enough. This perspective was very different from the one the nurse gave us at prenatal classes. She said that a newborn baby would be demanding and that more than likely we would need to adjust our expectations.

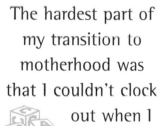

The hardest part of my transition to motherhood was that I couldn't clock out when I needed to.

We just didn't know how much we would have to change, since parenthood was too far removed from anything we had experienced. I thought, *Of course we will have time to clean the house, mow the lawn, maintain the garden, catch up with friends, and enjoy the "family" experience!* I also hoped I would have more time to read and cook, two of my favorite pastimes. Clearly my expectations were unrealistic; I had underestimated the level of care a newborn baby (and in my case, the firstborn) required.

It wasn't only the time commitment that threw me off, however; it was also the depression of feeling inadequate. I had not anticipated the "baby blues," the low self-esteem that comes from lack of affirmation and a sense of overwhelming duties. I expected the baby to be happy and sleep well if I fed it, bathed it, and kept it warm. I expected that the warm, cozy bond I had with my son would be enough to satisfy my internal drives. When the baby wasn't happy, I worked harder and tried to keep busy to the point of exhaustion.

In our zeal as new parents, we gave Ben too much care. We overstimulated him, we constantly held him, we sang to him (Hadie, Hadie Ho, the great big elephant is so slow!), we would check on him if he slept too long and pick him up if he didn't settle quickly. After our second child, we laughed at how intense and extreme we were in the level of care and attention we gave to Ben. At the time, however, there was nothing funny about how worn out we were.

Our Comfortable World Fell Apart

I couldn't believe Natalie felt as though she was failing as a mother and I was doing a much better job with Ben. I thought I was doing terribly and that she was absolutely fantastic. I felt inadequate too—not only as a new dad but also as her husband. I was totally out of my depth when it came to parenting, and I sensed I was failing Natalie because no matter what I said or did, nothing seemed to help.

I thought Natalie would be happy, that our son would sleep, that I wouldn't feel so clumsy. I thought that getting up wouldn't annoy me, that Natalie and I would be closer, that we wouldn't be so moody. We may not have expected to be perfect, but the reality was pretty dismal.

Our true downfall, however, was not our parenting skills; it was in failing to adjust our expectations once we saw our comfortable world falling apart. It was difficult for us to assess what our expectations should have been—we'd never done this before, and many of our friends had had an easy time coping with their newborns. For example, one of our friends arrived home from the hospital with her newborn son, and he slept so well that she had time and the energy to paint the windows and doorframes of her house.

> I thought that getting up wouldn't annoy me, that Natalie and I would be closer, that we wouldn't be so moody. We may not have expected to be perfect, but the reality was pretty dismal.

We were happy for our friend, but Natalie couldn't even imagine having time to paint her fingernails, let alone the house—she was too busy surviving.

Avoid the Comparison Pit

While it is easy to fall into the trap of comparing ourselves to other people or to what we think relatives and friends will expect of us, it is even easier to believe that transitioning from paid employment to caring for a baby is just like finishing one project and commencing work on a new one. People figure that because they have a track record of being competent managers in one area, their skills and experience will automatically bring about the same results in uncharted territory. How wrong that can be!

We made a lot of mistakes, despite having a supporting family, great prenatal information, and lots of friends who had done the baby thing well. But it didn't matter what advice people gave us; we had to go through the journey ourselves—hills, valleys, and all!

Nevertheless, we want to offer some advice that may help you avoid some of the potholes along the way. Who knows, you may not be as stubborn as we were. Our first bit of advice is don't be too hard on yourselves. Glenn's perception of how he was coping was totally different from how Natalie thought he was doing, and vice versa. Remind yourself that your baby's sleep pattern has nothing to do with whether you are a good parent. If you're having a hard time coping with a chronically crying baby, work out how to give each other a break. If you're on your own for a time, put on some music and earphones, or call a friend to come around and help alleviate the pressure. A baby who cries for long periods will wear anybody's patience down.

Our second recommendation is that you don't smother your baby with attention. Your friends and family may not have the courage to tell you that you might be overattentive to the needs of your baby. To keep perspective, remind yourself that your world doesn't have to shrink and be totally consumed by your baby.

Share how you are feeling with your spouse and discuss ways of relieving each other or helping each other get out of the house and be with friends. It's amazing how much bigger and exciting your world becomes after a little rest and hearing vocabulary that goes beyond goo-goo and ga-ga!

The third piece of advice is to hold on to the fact that you are on a journey (albeit only just beginning) and that you will get through to the end. That end might seem to be a long way off (eighteen years or so), but in reality, each day and every week is pretty much a milestone. You have survived!

Quick Tips

- If you haven't already done so, find time to sit down together and talk about your expectations and those of your spouse. Are they realistic? One activity we learned from prenatal classes was agreeing on a list of tasks that were important and making a note of the ones that weren't. For example, clothes washing and housecleaning have to be done every day, but we'd rather buy prepared meals than cook from scratch.

- Break down some of your new caring responsibilities into small projects to give you a sense of accomplishment after completing them. Believe it or not, bathing the baby, folding the diapers, and playing with your newborn are great achievements.

- You think your world has shrunk to fit inside a stroller. Talk to some friends who have toddlers or older children and find out what they did to make their world a little bigger.

"Discretion will watch over you,
and understanding will guard you." [2]

CHAPTER 4

We Can't Afford It!

I had just arrived home from the grocery store after purchasing a few items Natalie had requested. I expected a hero's welcome for saving her an errand. Plus, I had a surprise for her!

"How much did you spend at the supermarket?" Natalie asked when I entered the living room.

"I don't know, around sixty dollars."

"Sixty dollars!" she answered. "You were only supposed to spend around thirty."

"I know, I know," I said, thinking fast to find a way to appease her. "But I bought a few extra things and some chocolate—I thought we could spoil ourselves tonight. Wouldn't it be nice to focus on us for awhile?"

She gave me an exasperated look and said, "We can't afford it! I've worked so hard to save and buy the things we need, and now you've made things a lot harder. It's not fair. I go without little luxuries, but you can't help yourself."

Money Matters

Like us, you may find that adding a member to your family adds stress to your financial budget and to your relationship. Not only do new parents have to purchase quite a number of necessities, but they often have to accomplish this goal with one less income because of maternity leave or the loss of a job.

The list of things we needed to spend money on seemed to grow beyond anything we had expected. We wanted to redecorate, so we bought sandpaper, paintbrushes, paint, and wallpaper to prepare the nursery. The list included items such as a changing table, a set of drawers for the baby's clothes, a bassinet, bedding, diapers, wipes, baby clothes, and a small selection of soft toys. When you're shopping, you may find some quiet, reflective, meditative CDs to add to your collection—not for you, but for your baby!

With the inside of the house covered, we then needed equipment for leaving the house—a stroller, a child seat for the car, and a good-sized carry bag that would be sufficient to hold spare diapers, wipes, bibs, and a change of clothes.

As baby got older, we'd also need a high chair, a cot, a more mobile stroller, a couple of milk bottles, feeding utensils, and, yes, more toys. Now, with three children, we've discovered that the list never actually ends.

Needs vs. Wants

Natalie and I found ourselves falling into that trap of wanting to buy everything we thought either we would need or that our newborn baby might like. "Why don't you wait to see if you need it first?" Natalie's mother would say. "Somebody else might buy it for you" or "That's the difference today compared to our generation—we would buy it when we needed it if we could afford it. You don't wait. You just go out and buy it."

Natalie has always been better at managing the family budget than I. She's the one who makes sure that there's enough money in the bank to pay the bills when they're due, or that we can afford to buy something when we need it. Her ability to manage this area well

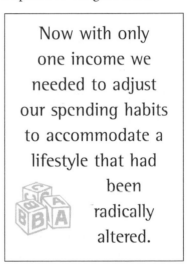

Now with only one income we needed to adjust our spending habits to accommodate a lifestyle that had been radically altered.

and my tendency to step over the spending boundaries occasionally created some tensions in our relationship, especially in the time leading up to and just after Ben's birth.

Natalie was justifiably concerned that we had been racking up a lot of purchases and expenses, and still had the normal household bills, mortgage payments, and running expenses for our car. Now with only one income we needed to adjust our spending habits to accommodate a lifestyle that had been radically altered from the one we had known.

Penny Pinching

Working out how to spend money on luxuries—like the chocolate—was one area we found especially challenging. For example, when and how frequently should we buy prepared meals to remove the stress of having to cook dinner? Spending more for "easy" food was a practical way to alleviate some stress in the housework area; however, that stress transferred itself to the area of our finances. We really had to think carefully before making a purchase; otherwise, when we really felt we needed something we may not have had the money to buy it. Only then would we look back and regret that we had too quickly and impulsively spent money we could have used more effectively.

This is how Natalie experienced our financial pressures:

The whole issue of having enough money is something I constantly struggled with. Although we had been anticipating dropping to one income, it came as a bit of a shock when the moment arrived when my fortnightly wage was no longer deposited into my bank account. Even though we had worked hard to reduce our mortgage payments while I was working, I suddenly felt more vulnerable financially. What if something went wrong? What if Glenn lost his job?

It seemed we had been spending money getting everything ready for our firstborn baby as if there were an endless supply. My mind shifted into a spending gear when I began to think about what my newborn would need. The maternal instinct to provide often overrode my financial sensibilities. Spending the money on my baby was one way to show how much I wanted and loved him.

After he was born, I wanted Ben to look nice for all of the visitors who would be admiring him in the days and weeks ahead. I was constantly looking out for clothes to buy Ben. I am sure that I easily spent double the amount of money on Ben's clothes compared to my own. Add to this the enormous quantity of diapers a newborn uses, and you have a substantial expense to cover. My needs were relegated to below my newborn's needs; he needed clothes, and I could go without. Even when I intentionally went shopping to buy some clothes for myself, it wasn't unusual for me to come home with clothes for Ben instead. Glenn couldn't understand this.

> Suddenly being financially vulnerable added to my stress level and made me realize more and more my life was out of control.

This was new territory for me; I had never needed to think about spending money on a newborn, other than buying a gift for a baby shower. Additionally, while we had two incomes, I didn't have to be so concerned about every purchase. It took awhile to develop discipline. Suddenly being financially vulnerable added to my stress level and made me realize more and more my life was out of control and changing. Concluding my nine-year career that had provided so much satisfaction, fulfillment, and financial security left me feeling lost and helpless. No longer contributing to our family finances caused me to panic when the bank balance plummeted. In an attempt to counterattack, I became vigilant about how much money Glenn and I spent each week and, therefore, frustrated when I would learn he had withdrawn money to buy clothes for himself and neglected to tell me.

A Balanced Budget

There were a number of things that helped us through this expensive period—the major one was being willing to work toward a modified budget to give us a better idea about what to expect, as well as identify which parts of the budget we needed to change. The second one was understanding that we didn't have to buy everything for our newborn son. Friends from work chipped in to help us with the diaper expense. Family members and friends often came bearing gifts that we had already bought in advance— if only we had waited! The third thing that helped was realizing that by adjusting our spending habits and not feeling pressured to buy everything, we could manage on a lot less money than we had before. Weighing up what was really important versus "what would be nice" helped us be much more sensible and prudent with our finances.

The lessons we learned in those first weeks have helped us raise our three children. We didn't always make the right choices, but we learned from our mistakes. When we overspent the budget, we just had to accept the fact that there were some things we wanted that we just couldn't have. The reality of that principle still applies today. Being aware of what things we could afford to live without, deciding carefully what we really needed, and saving until we had the money have helped us to be a lot more sensible about our finances. We discovered that a little planning (and sticking to it) can stretch our money a lot further.

Quick Tips

- Talk to other couples about how they would have prepared themselves better financially for having children—get ideas from them about what to include in a budget and try putting those ideas to work before the baby arrives.
- Talk to the soon-to-be grandparents and other family members about what gifts they can buy that you most need and may not be in a position to purchase yourselves.
- Not everything has to be new! Check out what other family members and friends may have that they no longer need, and offer to buy them. Don't be embarrassed to accept hand-me-downs. Also, you might check eBay (http://www.ebay.com) or your local newspaper for items people are trying to sell.

- If your friends ask you how they can help you the most, ask them to prepare some meals that can be frozen and used when you need them—not only does it take away the stress of having to prepare them, but it also reduces your grocery bill.

"The ant . . . prepares
its provisions in summer;
it gathers its food during harvest."³

CHAPTER 5

The Power
of a Timely Word

I would like you to think that I responded sensitively to Natalie's needs and concerns each day after the baby was born. After all, I am a psychologist; I love her and truly want to be a good husband. I would like you to think that I nurtured her and cared sacrificially for the woman who bore my children. Unfortunately, the truth is quite different.

I didn't get much better with practice as a parenting-partner. By the time our third baby came along, I still wasn't ready for the trauma of going through the crying stage all over again. I naively thought we would be able to settle Chloe much easier than our first two children. My frustration built, and as I had when the first two were infants, I took my anger out in words.

I still remember forcefully telling Natalie how much Chloe's crying bothered me and that I couldn't tolerate it for too long. I wish now that I had not been that insensitive. This venting only placed Natalie under greater pressure to respond as quickly as possible to our daughter's cries so that I wouldn't be so irritated by them. Although we both shared the role of quieting our daughter, it was difficult finding that balance between letting Chloe learn to calm herself at night and responding when she was truly distressed. Because I have a lower tolerance for the wailing than Natalie has, I made this balance even more difficult to reach. Natalie was pressured to pick up Chloe even when it might have been best to let her cry a bit longer.

This led to tension in our relationship that resulted in short outbursts of anger and irritation. What surprised us was that even though we loved each other and our daughter, we particularly resented those nighttime interruptions and we would turn into snarling adversaries. Out of exasperation and fatigue, we discovered the "art" of saying hurtful things to each other that only worsened the problem.

When Natalie told me that she was tired after a long day caring for our children, I found myself reacting and becoming defensive. Was she suggesting that my day had been a lot easier? Was this her way of hinting that it would be nice if I could help out a little more? The conversations would go something like this:

"Glenn, do you mind bathing Ben and getting him ready for bed while I take a breather?"

"You've got to be joking," I replied. "I've just come home from working a long day and now you want me to work another shift while you take a break! When do I get to take a rest?" (Sound familiar?)

What's So Funny?

Then there were those lighter moments when Natalie and I were too slow to put the diaper on, only to find ourselves frantically trying to stem the flow that was shooting all over the place, or finding a spot of spit-up on a freshly ironed shirt when rushing to leave the house. Other times we must have looked terrible after a sleepless night, but we soldiered on, ignoring the questioning looks of others. I remember a number of Saturday morning experiences when we put Ben in the stroller and walked down to the local shops only to see people give that knowing smile that says, "Those poor parents. They've obviously been up all night."

It was easy for us to laugh at those more public scenes, but much more difficult to see the lighter moments when one of us made a joke about something the other was doing—like putting the diaper on the wrong way or needing to spend double shower time just to wake up. Instead of laughing with each other at these peculiar moments, we reacted to the attempt at humor as if it were a putdown. Because we were so tired and needing reassuring encouragement, we became oversensitive to each other's words. Rather than laugh, we got upset and said things that drove an emotional wedge between us. The encouragement we should have given to each other was left unspoken. We were each so consumed by our fatigue and constant demands of the baby that our normal sensitivities were warped. Add to this our own feelings of inadequacy, and we discovered a recipe for frustration and tension in our relationship.

What I probably needed to hear from Natalie the most were words like "I think it's amazing how well you have adjusted to being a dad" and "I know you're tired, and I appreciate how hard it must be juggling work and home responsibilities, but I think you're doing a great job. I'm so proud of you." Because my perspective on things at home got distorted due to how tired and frustrated I could be, I needed reassurance that I wasn't doing as badly as I believed.

> Even people who are normally confident in many other areas struggle with the constant demands of caring for a newborn.

It's incredible how powerful and energizing it was to hear those sorts of words from Natalie.

Words Aren't Cheap

The words that I (Natalie) appreciated hearing most were those that told me how special our son was. Because a lot of my energy was being invested in caring for our baby, I needed to know that it was all worthwhile and that my caring was being rewarded. I wanted someone to love my baby the same way I did. I realize that this might sound strange, but when Glenn told me that our son was adorable, it affirmed what I was doing as worthwhile.

Even though we thought we had a relatively strong relationship, the stresses and challenges we experienced placed that relationship under great pressure during this time of parenting a newborn—even to the point where we wondered if our relationship would ever return to what it had once been.

Words Can Hurt—and Heal

There is no doubt that spoken words have the ability to hurt us, or encourage us and make us feel better about a challenging situation.

Hearing encouraging words that affirm us are vital in this early stage of caring for a newborn, because there are so many questions, concerns, and mistakes we have made, and all of these factors impact our caring ability and our relationship with our spouse.

It certainly is not unusual for parents of a newborn—especially if this is their first child—to question their ability to read all the signs correctly and know the most appropriate response. Even people who are normally confident in many other areas struggle with the constant demands of caring for a newborn and the many lifestyle changes that parenthood brings.

The list of lifestyle changes may seem endless—parenting skills to learn, things you have to borrow or buy, a house or room that needs to be altered, and a shopping list that looks vastly different from the one you were used to before you had a baby. You may even have had to ask somebody at the supermarket where to find the baby products aisle! Although there have been moments to treasure (the first smile, the wonder of baby cooing), you feel they have been outweighed by the many adjustments you've had to make.

> Constantly questioning your value as a parent saps your energy level.

In all of this you may have been putting yourself through an exhaustive checklist that tells you that you are either a good parent or a bad one. Constantly questioning your value as a parent saps your energy level.

A timely word of encouragement or affirmation is something that your husband or wife desperately needs from you. It's important to realize that paying a compliment is not the same as flattery. Flattery is often insincere and manipulative. A compliment affirms and genuinely seeks to build up your mate. It may even be as simple as letting your spouse know that you are amazed at her staying power when others would have given up, or it might be letting the baby's father know how impressed you have been with his efforts.

Words are powerful. Your words have the potential to hurt and crush your spouse's spirit, or they can bring hope, encouragement, refreshment, and healing.

Quick Tips

- What words would your husband or wife most appreciate hearing from you right now?
- Ask yourself, "What things have I been saying that may not be helpful to my spouse?"
- In a practical way, explore how you might be able to alleviate some of your spouse's fears and anxieties.

"There is one who speaks rashly
like a piercing sword;
but the tongue of the wise
[brings] healing."[4]

CHAPTER 6

A Rude Awakening

W*ah* . . . *wah* . . . *wah* . . . *wah* . . .
I had no idea how long a baby could cry! Coming
from the relative comfort of a home without baby noises, this was
a rude awakening—literally. Apart from my teenage years when I
went through the mandatory period of listening to loud music,
the word *decibels* took on a whole new meaning.

I remember Natalie asking me, "What else did you expect?"
To be truthful I didn't exactly know. Sure, I knew any newborn
would cry, but it couldn't be that difficult to settle Ben. Maybe it
was a guy thing. I soon wished there was an "on and off" switch
or that it was simply a matter of taking out the batteries when we
needed a break!

My sleep troubles began the very first night our son was born.
Our hospital provided the opportunity for couples to spend the

night together at the maternity ward with their new babies. I was suddenly faced with a huge dilemma. On the one hand I'm thinking: *How nice it would be to go home and stumble into bed and get a good night's rest. After all, I need to build up my energy reserves for tomorrow!* But on the other: *I've got to keep up appearances because it actually wasn't me that experienced the physical rigors of labor, and, of course, I don't want to be accused of being insensitive.*

I decided to stay the night. As far as pleasing Natalie, this was a wise choice. As far as my body was concerned, it was practically suicide, because even though Natalie was tired, her adrenaline was still pumping and she couldn't stop jabbering happily about the arrival of our son. Before I knew it, it was time to get up. Natalie reminded me that in the weeks ahead I'd appreciate those precious few minutes of rest I was able to snatch!

She was right. Sleeping past eight o'clock in the morning was a thing of the past, and I didn't need to worry about hearing my alarm go off—it didn't matter; Ben's cries overrode my snooze button. Being awakened in the mornings by a baby screaming for attention wasn't so bad, but after having already been up at midnight, disturbed at 2:00 A.M., forced to crawl out of bed at 4:00 A.M., and then somehow finding my son while barely awake at 6:00 A.M. was overkill.

Life as a Zombie

This exhaustion, this zombie-like existence, this never-ending "screamfest"—this is no dream. You are a parent. You do have a baby. And yes, you're feeling very tired.

Whereas last week you wanted to know what on earth you had done to yourself by having a baby; a week later you know exactly what you've done. What you didn't know back then was exactly how tired you would be this week. It's not that you weren't told. It was more that the warnings didn't appear on your radar screen because it was so far removed from your experience. It doesn't matter how many people tell you how you will feel, you tend to think they're either exaggerating or that their coping skills aren't quite as good as yours.

Our son did not settle quickly at night and fall into those beautiful deep sleeps that we were hoping for. For us the opposite was true. Our son would eventually drift off

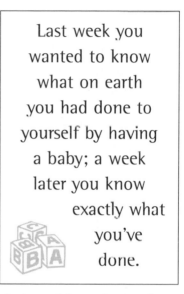

Last week you wanted to know what on earth you had done to yourself by having a baby; a week later you know exactly what you've done.

to sleep between eleven and twelve o'clock at night, only to wake four or five times, and sometimes more, to eat or to be comforted. This *un*-sleeping pattern began to cause quite a bit of tension between us.

For us, it got worse before it got better.

Sleeping Tigers

Here's a picture of what was going on in our relationship:

While Natalie has always been a sound sleeper, I am definitely a light sleeper. I wake at the slightest noise and take awhile to get back to sleep. With a newborn who didn't sleep well, I discovered one of the significant downsides of being a light sleeper. I heard every snore, gurgle, and sigh my son made, causing me to wake up more frequently than I had hoped, and certainly more often than Natalie, who amazingly slept through it all—even the cries. Wow, she was a great sleeper! Or was she?

> I became rather perplexed when she began to over-state how many times she got up at night to attend to our son and under- state the number of times I had.

I soon caught on she had sometimes pretended to be asleep in the hope that I would promptly attend to Ben's screaming. Once I was up, however, what was I to do? It wasn't my breasts he wanted. He wanted something only his mother could give him. It seemed that my getting up wasn't very productive since Natalie had to wake up anyway.

To her family, Natalie has always been known as The Count. She has this remarkable ability to keep score of things. She always knows how many helpings of dessert I have eaten or how many Australian chocolate cookies I devour while having a cup of coffee, and she certainly knows when any money has recently gone missing from her purse. I really don't like to admit it, but most of the time she is right!

After the first few nights of being home with a newborn, though, I seriously began to question her mathematical ability. I became rather perplexed when she began to overstate how many times she got up at night to attend to our son and understate the number of times I had.

In your case, this may not seem like a big issue. But hang on a minute! If I was losing valuable sleep and getting up three or four more times than Natalie, I wanted her to know that I was "doing my bit" and had a legitimate reason for being tired. I soon realized, however, that Natalie counted incorrectly because she didn't always wake up when I took care of Ben.

Very soon we were both counting, comparing, and deciding whose turn it was to get up. "It must be your turn," moaned Natalie as she pulled the covers up over her head.

"You've got to be kidding! I've been up three times already," I replied in a voice that sounded like somebody barely alive.

"I got up last time, and besides, if I go, Ben will only smell my milk and want to nurse," complained Natalie. And so it went on, until one of us begrudgingly relented.

What resulted was the development of a game that was quite destructive. Instead of looking for ways to support and help each other, we began to focus more on our own needs. I began to feel as though I was the one that got a raw deal when it came to needing more sleep and time out, whereas Natalie felt the same way about herself.

Of course, how we felt about this "game" and its impact on us was considerably influenced by our exhaustion. The tiredness led to shorter fuses, unpleasant exchanges, and unresolved tensions. Apart from being totally dissatisfied with how we were dealing with our situation and how it was hurting our relationship, we knew we had to resolve it because tiredness was going to be part of our journey for quite awhile longer.

Wake-Up Call

Here's Natalie's verse of the same song:

I love my sleep. Before Ben and I came home from the hospital I had asked a lot of my friends about what techniques they found worked in getting their babies to sleep. I felt that if I followed their advice, then I would also have a baby that slept well. Was I wrong! While we were still in the hospital, I had a strong inkling that I was going to be in for some challenges. Even the nursing staff had difficulties settling Ben at night. Poor Glenn. Some nights when he came to see me and Ben in the hospital, he had to look after Ben while I tried getting some sleep.

I was certainly a lot more stressed about caring for a newborn than I thought I would be. Normally I am a very practical person, but with Ben, I'm not sure what went wrong; I became quite irrational at times. I desperately clung to every idea that somebody offered in the hope that sleepless nights and days would end quickly—listening to soothing music, giving him a hot bath every night, attending to him every time he cried, and so on.

Every day I looked forward to nighttime, when I could have at least some break from Ben's demands. Although Glenn helped a lot at night and put forth superhuman effort, it was never enough. What I really needed was some space between Ben and me. Getting a few minutes to read a book in bed knowing that Glenn was looking after Ben felt like heaven! When it didn't happen, I found myself resenting Ben. After all, I had given him all of my time and energy during the day. All I asked for in return was a little space and four to six hours of unbroken sleep. It wasn't that I didn't love Ben. I merely found that nothing of me was left.

I also didn't like the way that the lack of sleep and resulting frustrations changed the way Glenn and I related to each other. We had an excellent relationship, and communication was central to that. Seemingly overnight, this was gone. Early on I think we both hoped that the next night things would improve, but when the next night arrived, and then the next, and still no change, we realized that it was going to be this way for some time.

Friends and family offered help, but I felt too proud to accept it. Accepting their help would prove that I was inadequate. I didn't like being dependent on other people.

Fatigue Kills

Have you ever driven past one of those signs on the roadside that says "Fatigue Kills. Slow Down"? It's a fairly blunt message and one that requires no explanation.

Similarly, fatigue can "kill" a relationship. In caring for a newborn, there are constant demands on your physical and emotional reserves. Before you know it, you can be so physically and emotionally exhausted that your words are no longer measured and your reactions to your husband's words and actions (or lack thereof) can become swift.

The unfortunate thing that happens here is that your tiredness increases your stress levels, and your rising stress levels affect the way you communicate and respond to each other.

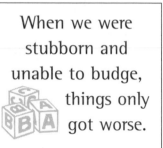

When we were stubborn and unable to budge, things only got worse.

Tiredness doesn't occur only from not getting as much sleep as you would like; it's also from the pressure of maintaining all of those day-to-day responsibilities that have become part of your life and were part of your stress before the baby: preparing meals, washing clothes, keeping the house clean, doing the ironing, paying the bills, trying to find time when you can catch up with friends and family members, and the list goes on. It also includes your spouse going off to work and leaving you completely responsible for the care of your new baby.

Tiredness can also result from what at first appears to be reasonable expectations, but they haven't been adjusted to accommodate how you and your spouse are feeling and coping with the stresses and challenges of caring for a newborn. It can be the stress of not getting through as many tasks as you wanted to that makes you feel guilty and inadequate or causes you to feel even more tired.

Recognizing this destructive cycle and working with each other to minimize the stress is an important step in overcoming the impact tiredness can have on your relationship. When we're fatigued, we are more likely to react hastily to our husband or wife. Giving thought to your responses is the next step in making sure that tiredness will not kill your relationship or negatively affect the way you respond to your baby and its needs.

Learning to compromise was important. When we were stubborn and unable to budge, things only got worse. One way we compromised was to structure our nights in a way that allowed each of us to get a block of uninterrupted sleep (or at least assured we didn't have to get up for awhile).

"This isn't working," Natalie would say.

"I agree. We're both exhausted, and it's not getting easier," I might say back.

"Why don't I give Ben to you once I've given him his evening feed, allowing me to get some sleep, seeing as you're a night person anyway?" Natalie would suggest.

And so we'd work it out.

We hope you find it encouraging that our relationship did survive the phenomenon of sleep deprivation, and that eventually when we turned the corner and rediscovered the joys of sleep, a healthy relationship began to materialize once again. We learned that open, honest, and forgiving communication was the key to moving beyond these challenges. A lot of prayer also helped us over the line!

Quick Tips

- Understand each other's need for sleep and space, and agree on how you can schedule caring responsibilities to give each other a break. As much as possible, try swapping the tasks you are responsible for on weekends.

- Although it's important to work on affirming and encouraging each other, what gives your words substance is when you can relieve each other practically—arrange family help, or have the grandparents look after your child while you and your spouse do the shopping or go out for a quick dinner.

- Learn how to reach a compromise to prevent your situation from becoming more desperate and your reactions to each other more defensive.

"Love covers all offenses."[5]

CHAPTER 7

Recharge Your
Spouse's Batteries

This may seem like an unusual subject to address when the
last thing you feel like doing is focusing on how you can en-
ergize each other. But it's at this time, when your energy levels are
at a record low, that you need to support each other the most. It
is good to consider how you are going to be able to help each other
go the distance and not leave the other one behind, physically,
emotionally, and spiritually.

One of the things we learned about ourselves even before we
had a baby was what time of the day we functioned best and what
activities recharged our batteries.

Here's Glenn's perspective:

I am definitely a night person and prefer not to turn off the lights at a time when I am still wide awake and have plenty of energy. Natalie, on the other hand, is a morning person. Whereas I struggle to pull back the blankets early in the morning and drag myself to the shower, Natalie will generally find it easy to get out of bed and be ready to start her day. Before the baby, she was getting up when I thought an extra hour in bed would be nice, and I was still going strong at night when she was ready to fall into bed—gone were the university days when I could burn the candle at both ends!

What did this mean? We evaluated our natural strengths and created a schedule that would maximize our effectiveness. It meant that I was able to handle caring for our baby boy at night, while Natalie was far more capable in the morning. Naturally this didn't always work out exactly the same way each day, as we soon learned that there would be quite a few exceptions where nights would seemingly merge into days and vice versa.

Give Each Other Space

Understanding the things that recharged our batteries was also a great help in understanding how we could assist each other. If there was one area where we were similar, it was in the area of just simply needing some personal space to catch our breath—in other words, being able to find a place where we could individually relax without the pressure of having to attend to a baby or feel as though we should be helping the other.

Where we were a little different was Natalie enjoyed curling up on the bed and reading a novel, while Glenn enjoyed sitting down and reading the newspaper over a strong cup of coffee— either down at the local café or at home. As Glenn travels frequently for work, he enjoys lounging around at home whereas Natalie would much rather get out of the house.

A Piece of Heaven

Natalie recalls a time when Glenn went the extra mile:

I remember one night when my friend Lois called me and said she was going to come and take me out for coffee. Ignoring my objections she just turned up at the front door and said, "I know you don't want to go, but you're coming!" What I didn't realize then was Glenn had called Lois during the day from work and shared his concern that he couldn't get me out of the house at a time when I desperately needed a break. Although I was initially upset at him for doing this, I did appreciate his thoughtfulness.

On a number of occasions I remember how Glenn would choose to get up during the night to sit with me while I breast-fed Ben, just to keep me company. It also felt like a piece of heaven when early in the morning Glenn would bring our waking, hungry son to me, and then take him back to burp him, wrap him, and settle him back to sleep. This was particularly nice during those cold winter months.

Share the Load

I have to say that the energizing certainly wasn't all one-way. On some weekends Natalie would get up in the morning (remember, she is a morning person!) and take our son down to the bakery to pick up some bread and buy a newspaper. What more could I ask for? Freshly baked bread, the newspaper—with the latest football scores—and a freshly ground and brewed cup of coffee. Now that's what I call energizing!

> Most people's batteries are recharged when they see what positive effect they are having on someone else.

Natalie also tried to make my nights as easy as possible once I arrived home from work. Knowing that it wasn't long before I took over the reins and looked after our son while Natalie got some rest, she would try to have dinner prepared. These efforts enabled us to effectively share the load between us and keep our energy at a reasonable level.

Another way we worked toward this goal was breaking the night into evening and early morning shifts. As I was a night person, I would take responsibility for attending to our son's needs between dinner and midnight. Natalie on the other hand would take over between midnight and 6:00 A.M. I would do my best to allow Natalie to spend some extra time lying in bed on Saturday morning, while she would do the same for me on Sunday morning. While there were definitely a few exceptions, it generally worked well.

A Refreshing Change

What energizes you? How do you recharge your batteries? What gets you excited or makes you feel good? Believe it or not, most people's batteries are recharged when they see what positive effect they are having on someone else—there is true joy in giving. Generally, it's also much easier to help someone else when you know that they have gone out of their way to assist you.

Similarly, helping and supporting your spouse at this time will ultimately bring refreshment to you as well. When your spouse is refreshed, she will be in a much better position to refresh you. When she is feeling renewed, she will be less stressed and tired, and able to cope better with the demands of this challenging parenting phase. She'll enjoy being a mom more, and hopefully break the fatigue cycle that leads to such dissatisfaction. This also helps to create a better environment for the both of you in coming to terms with your new roles.

Plan how you can go about refreshing your spouse—order some takeout or offer to cook. Buy a special gift or send flowers. Offer to give your wife or husband the night off. You'll be amazed at the difference it will make!

Quick Tips

- Share with each other what energizes and refreshes you.
- Commit to at least one thing you will do in the next day or two that will refresh each other.
- While you don't want to fall into the trap of keeping score of how many times you are energizing your spouse, you do want to be honest about your expectations.

"He who refreshes others
will himself be refreshed."[6]

CHAPTER 8

How Can They All Be Right?

The wisdom of our parents was never quite so evident as it was when our first son was around eight months old and still not sleeping well. Natalie and Ben booked into a baby sleep clinic that provides respite for the sleep-deprived mother and helps young parents establish a healthier sleeping pattern for the baby. This was an absolute godsend!

We couldn't help but notice, however, that all of the techniques we learned at the baby sleep clinic were totally in line with what Natalie's mother had been saying all along. We could have taken her advice from the beginning and saved ourselves a lot of sleepless nights.

But would Mother always be right? Should we take her advice about everything, even if it was inconsistent with what the doctors said? There was so much to learn about caring for a newborn. How do amateurs go about the business of parenting?

Worry, Worry, Worry

I (Natalie) remember how confused I was after arriving home from the hospital with our son. Months in advance I prepared for this moment so that there wouldn't be many surprises when we got home. I committed to learn as much as possible by reading books my friends had recommended. I soon selected my favorites, which I made sure were by my bedside when I wanted to double-check something.

> Tension between us came to a head when, five weeks after his birth, Ben needed an operation.

Being a worrier, I found myself reading all the books on a particular issue. If any of them said something slightly different I began to worry about which one I could trust. Not that the issues were necessarily of a major nature, but being an inexperienced mother I wanted to make sure that nothing potentially harmful escaped my attention. Some of those issues were simply "Was the belly button healing sufficiently or was it possibly infected?" "Is that diaper rash or thrush?" and "Is his breathing normal or slightly irregular?"

Glenn on the other hand is not much of a worrier. This occasionally causes tension in our relationship. In order to correct my worrying, he tends to go to the other end of the spectrum and say things like "Everything will be all right" or "Don't worry. Let's just see how things go over the next few days." I didn't always find his responses very reassuring (which is often all I need) and began to worry more.

This tension between us came to a head when, five weeks after his birth, Ben needed an operation to repair two hernias. Unfortunately, infection set in not long after we brought Ben home. I would ask Glenn if he thought the area was infected, and he would respond that it looked quite normal and that I was over-reacting. Only eventually did he agree with me that it didn't look like it was improving, and we took Ben to the doctors where we learned that he had staph—a hospital-acquired infection, which is fairly serious.

I felt as though I had let Ben down by not taking him to the doctors earlier. As a result I became angry at myself for not trusting my own judgment and angry at Glenn because he wasn't as responsive to my concerns as he could have been.

Although he was only trying to keep my worrying in perspective, I would have felt better if he could have at least acknowledged my concern as rational and validate how I was feeling. What I really needed from him was some thoughtful, realistic responses to my concerns.

Overwhelming Advice

One of the fears of leaving the hospital was knowing that there were no nurses or medical staff at home who could answer our questions and give us the reassurance we often needed.

Leaning on the support of family and friends provided an interesting dilemma for us. Naturally we were eager to look after our baby the way that we wanted to, when we wanted to. At the same time, however, we didn't want to unintentionally turn help away by making others feel uncomfortable around us, even if they were quick to point out how they would do things differently.

At times we felt overwhelmed by advice. Here's how Glenn describes it:

We soon discovered that our parents and friends had a lot of advice to give. The ironic thing was that our parents thought some of the procedures we learned in prenatal classes were ridiculous. "We never did it that way, and you survived, didn't you?" Natalie's mom would say. I still remember our mothers coming along to an "Induction Day for Grandparents" conducted by the hospital as part of our prenatal training classes. They laughed together about "how times have changed!" "I raised six of you," my mother would say, "and you all survived sleeping on your side, not your back. Furthermore, I used to wrap you all up tightly, not like the nurse is telling you to do."

Although we were determined to learn how to be good parents by trying different things ourselves, it was still comforting to know that our parents were there as a backup if Plan A or B failed. Fortunately, neither of our moms was inclined to say, "I told you so." After raising three infants, I now realize they could have said, "I told you he was unsettled at night because he was cold," or "You overstimulate him."

When we did eventually learn that our parents had been right, we were mad at ourselves for taking so long to find out. So much anxiety, stress, and frustration could have been avoided.

Does Mother Know Best?

We may sound ungrateful for the advice we were given. Certainly that was not the case! We appreciated our parents' and friends' concern and wisdom tremendously. What we found difficult, however, was that everybody seemed to have a different view, and we weren't sure who was right. We also didn't want to offend anybody by ignoring well-intended advice and choosing to do things differently.

> "I don't know who is right; my mother says one thing, and then the nurse or doctor says something completely different!"

The support and advice offered by family, friends, and parents can create tension in your relationship if you don't talk about it with each other. We found that we needed to be careful in the way we responded to each other, especially if conflicting suggestions were made by our parents. Here's how Natalie felt:

One time we were having some challenges with Ben's feeding habits. The hospital staff encouraged me to feed Ben as many times as he wanted it; my mother told me that his minisnacks would just make me more tired and reinforce a bad habit.

"I don't know who is right; my mother says one thing, and then the nurse or doctor says something completely different!" Glenn wasn't as concerned about this as I was, and he didn't even look up from reading the newspaper when I expressed my dilemma. But I could have used some reassurance and some confidence that I could be a good mother. I didn't want to hurt my mother by not listening to her, but I also didn't want to make a mistake.

> I felt that my mothering ability was on trial, and I was determined to pass the test.

I wish I could have relaxed a bit more. Lying in bed late at night exhausted, we had numerous discussions about why I felt the need to be in control as much as I did. Ultimately, it came down to two things. The first one is personality (the way I am wired). I tend to think along the lines of "What if things don't go right?" or "What will someone think if this happens?" I wanted to be prepared for every possibility.

The second reason I had trouble making decisions about Ben was that I felt a need to prove to myself and to others that I was a capable and competent mother. If my friends could succeed at motherhood, then I should be able to as well. I felt that my mothering ability was on trial, and I was determined to pass the test and achieve the status of "experienced mother."

Take Some Advice

We missed out on receiving a lot of support being offered because we didn't swallow our pride. During those crisis moments, we didn't even realize we were being foolish. How bad can it really be if you let your determined family members and friends help out? If the advice isn't potentially harmful, why not give it a whirl?

You may be surprised to find out that babies can still go to sleep while you go about your normal daily routine, even if it involves vacuuming your baby's bedroom, as Lisa (one of Natalie's friends) advised. With our first baby, we tiptoed everywhere and the slightest noise woke him from his sleep. With our second child, we pretended as if he weren't asleep and were amazed when he continued to sleep no matter how much noise we made. After this discovery we certainly wished that we had taken heed to that bit of advice much sooner.

You may have parents who want to help but are keeping in the background, afraid that you will see their offer of assistance as interfering in your relationship. Even though it has been some time since your parents gave birth to you, in most cases they'll have some understanding of what you are going through.

It would be helpful to discuss with them how you would need their support and where you would value their help the most. This way, they know they are needed, but you have set some boundaries. And importantly, you have defused a situation that could place your relationship with your spouse under more stress.

Quick Tips

- When evaluating advice, make sure you listen to and respect the views of your spouse, even if you disagree. Before an issue arises, discuss areas you feel strongly about.

- In determining what advice you want to accept, agree on it as a couple. If necessary, explain to your parents or friends why you are choosing advice contrary to theirs.

- Discuss with your parents and friends what practical support you would appreciate the most. Don't offend relatives by refusing all help. Let them know what you really need, such as help with the washing, cleaning the house, cooking, babysitting, or merely keeping you company while your spouse is gone.

"Let the wise listen
and add to their learning, and let
the discerning get guidance."[7]

CHAPTER 9

Slipping Standards

I (Glenn) grew up in a family of six children and two extremely competent parents. Mom was rarely flustered in keeping the routine at home on track—even when she catered for the endless number of visitors that were invited home for dinner. Mom was the type of person who was able to remain calm in a crisis and always keep her head. The remarkable thing about this was she had a wonderful sense of humor and always enjoyed having people around her.

When I was seventeen, for example, I arrived home with a broken wrist after playing British Bulldog on roller skates. She wrapped my wrist with a bandage and told me it would be better in the morning. I'm sure she thought she knew more about my injury than I did, and that she would be proved right. After moaning for a day, I finally convinced her I was in agony and she took

me to the hospital. The nurse took one look at my wrist and ex-
claimed to my mother, "Well, obviously it's broken!" Only then
did I receive the sympathy I sought.

Somehow, Mom always managed six growing, demanding
children with considerable ease—at least that's how she appeared.
Dad complemented her efforts by always working hard, leading
various church activities, and generally making sure we weren't late
for things—he was always a stickler for being on time. Rarely did
I see my mother and father disagree or argue. They always seemed
to have everything under control. Rather than frustrate me, this
impressed me. Today as I look back with three children of my
own, I wonder how on earth my parents had so much energy to
care for others while maintaining their church activities and managing the six of us!

I expected to adjust quickly to parenthood; after all, my
mother and father coped with six of us, so surely I could cope with
one! And besides, I had always thought I was reasonably good at
being flexible and adjusting to new situations. I discovered, however, that when you have to think about the needs of your spouse
and your new baby, you can't simply just "go with the flow" all of
the time and deal with whatever comes when it happens. I knew
what it was like to start a new business, develop strategic plans,
present reports to a board, recruit and manage a team of people to
help me achieve the organization's goals, and maintain a busy
schedule . . . but nothing quite prepared me for the new (and re-
lentless) demands of a newborn. The effort Natalie and I put into
some of our "perfect" plans sometimes had to go by the wayside.

Evaluate Your Expectations

This frustration spilled over into our relationship, and we constantly had to evaluate whether our expectations were realistic. Sometimes they were. The problem was that Natalie and I had not communicated our expectations to each other. I might have looked forward to reading the newspaper on Saturday morning before reluctantly embarking on the list of household chores, while Natalie was hoping to get the chores out of the way so we could drive to her parents' place for lunch. We each assumed that the other would fit in with our own personal agenda.

Being a trained psychologist and having worked considerably with families, I set for myself a certain standard and had an image to maintain. What I didn't realize was just how difficult it would be to accomplish this when I was tired and feeling grumpy.

> Frustration spilled over into our relationship, and we constantly had to evaluate whether our expectations were realistic.

Not only was it challenging to demonstrate to everybody else that I was coping when I wasn't; it reinforced a lie that said to them that I didn't need them or their support. If there is one thing experience has taught me, it is that pretending everything is OK only creates pressure for others to maintain the same charade. I was making things more difficult than they should have been because I didn't allow my friends and family members to help me when they wanted to. Maybe it was just a guy thing. The things we inflict on ourselves!

When Winning the Battle
Means Losing the War

Normally, Glenn has a lot of energy, and I think he struggled a lot more than he expected to in providing the practical support I needed. In hindsight I think he did an incredible job! Going off to work after a bad night's sleep, coming home after work and needing to pitch in as soon as he got through the front door, and knowing that he was in for a long night must have really impacted him—especially when the same routine didn't differ much for the first few months. How he hung in there, I don't know. What I do know is that he thought the same about me. He knew how tired I was getting up at night to breast-feed and how much I struggled to accommodate the baby's routine. There were many times when out of sheer frustration caused by our tiredness, we would argue on autopilot.

This interchange was typical of our discussions:

"Do you mind checking on Ben before you turn out the light?" I asked once.

"Sure," Glenn replied. After a few moments he returned to tell me that Ben was asleep. "Do you mind if I read for a little while?"

"Why do you have to keep the light on?" I said. "I'm so tired and we've both got a chance here to get some sleep."

"Just for a little bit?"

"I can't believe you want to read when I'm so tired," I said, probably whining a bit.

"Well, this is my way to unwind," Glenn said, "Ten minutes is not going to hurt!"

At times like this, our conversation deteriorated and our dialogue became a tit for tat. What was probably a reasonable request became an all-consuming battle that each of us wanted to win.

Deep down I think we both struggled because we knew there were times when things between us should have been much better than they were, but we didn't seem to have the energy to address the problems. We also didn't want anybody else to know. We wanted them to see us coping, so that they would think we were good parents. When we were prepared to be a little vulnerable in front of our friends, we often discovered that many of them struggled just as much as we did, and, like us, they didn't want anyone else to think they were bad parents or perceive that their relationship was shaky.

Keeping Up Appearances

The unfortunate thing about keeping up appearances and pretending that everything was OK on the inside was that it led to two specific problems. The first was that it became increasingly difficult to maintain a charade—sometimes the pent-up emotion, the stress of doing everything ourselves, the weight of each other's expectations, the tiredness, the constancy of caring for

Ben and attending to his needs, and the frustration this placed on my relationship with Glenn was like a virtual time bomb ready to explode.

I'm sure Glenn was horrified from time to time when I disclosed how I was coping. He wasn't shocked because I was willing to share how I was feeling with my friends, but more because I occasionally told others about my perceptions of how he was helping or not helping without first talking to him about it!

> Deep down I think we both struggled because we knew there were times when things between us should have been much better.

I remember an occasion when we were sitting in our lounge room talking with some friends when the topic focused on the early weeks adjusting to a newborn. Steven and Lisa asked us how we were coping, and I think Glenn got a big shock when I said it had been trying because he wasn't able to help much. Glenn was embarrassed and got quite defensive as he tried to tell Steven and Lisa of all the different ways he was helping. In hindsight it was unfair for me to talk about Glenn like this, especially when he believed that he was doing the best he could. Although I didn't intend to hurt Glenn, being so exhausted, I was not as sensitive or careful with my words as I would have been under different circumstances.

The second problem with trying to keep up appearances was that I pushed away my friends and family members. I squashed some of their chances to get involved and enjoy our new and expanded family. As irrational as it was, I somehow believed that it was more important to create the illusion I was coping well than to allow people to be near us and possibly judge me a poor mother.

Perhaps one of the strangest pressures we both experienced in the first few weeks after coming home with a newborn was feeling the need to have it all together. This included knowing exactly what to do whenever it needed to be done, coping with unexpected events and surprises, and having our emotions under control at all times, even if on the inside we felt like exploding.

> As irrational as it was, I somehow believed that it was more important to create the illusion I was coping well than to allow people to be near us and possibly judge me a poor mother.

We found ourselves looking at others and comparing our situation and our parenting skills. This would happen while we were shopping, visiting friends who either had older babies or young toddlers, or at church. We seemed to be constantly mindful of what others might think about our baby or our emerging skills as parents.

The Secret No One Shares

Although bringing a baby home from the hospital is not one of the most peaceful transitions you'll encounter in life, it's important not to fall into the trap of comparing your experience with your friends and family members. Each of them may tell you what a wonderful time this is—and it is. They may say how blessed they were—and they were! Some of them believed that this was the moment when they felt they had become a family—and it may be for you, too.

You may hear all of these wonderful things and much more, but just underneath that layer are a host of other things you will rarely hear at the time. These might include being anxious about how they will cope in the days ahead, feeling uncertain about what to do or whom to turn to for advice, or wondering when they will be able to sleep.

It's not that these things didn't exist; they just didn't think it was important to tell you! To be fair to some of our friends, they just simply forgot how hard it was. Either time had eroded their memory, or simply, the joys of parenting outweighed the early sacrifices they made. Then again, imagine if they had remembered and been truthful in revealing all of the challenges and stresses of caring for a newborn—you might never have had a baby. (While that may be a tempting fantasy now—life with baby does get better.)

During this time of considerable change and perhaps fruitless search for sleep, comparing your parenting ability or your baby to someone else's is not likely to raise your energy levels. Everybody is different, everybody parents differently, and every baby is different. Some eat better and some eat irregularly. Some get colic, and others seemingly fall into a heavenly routine. Some parents cope well, and others don't. You'll feel more at peace, however, when you don't use up so much valuable energy trying to keep up appearances in front of everyone else, including your spouse.

Quick Tips

- Be honest with each other about how you are coping so that you don't overlook each other's need for support.
- Discuss ahead of time what you are willing to share about each other, your relationship, and your struggles in front of your friends and family.
- Be careful not to be too hard on yourself by comparing your situation to someone else's. Your emotional energy is better spent caring for your baby and supporting your spouse.

"A patient person [shows] great understanding, but a quick-tempered one promotes foolishness."[8]

CHAPTER 10

Whatever Happened to Fun?

Babies cry. They wee and poo and have gas. They wake you up when you're in a deep sleep, and they keep you awake when your body feels barely able to function. Babies seem to have this innate ability to either want your attention or demand to be fed just as you're about to sit down and eat your meal. Where's the fun in that? You discover the joyous relief of collapsing into a lounge chair or bed, only to be jolted moments later with the realization that your baby has roused from her brief slumber and is now screaming for your presence. Where's the fun in that?

Glenn remembers one particular day that wasn't much fun:

I can vividly recall the time I arrived home from work one evening. I was only barely able to make it through the front door before I was virtually gang-tackled by my two young boys, Ben and Ryan. My daughter, Chloe, who was about eight months old, had obviously watched the entire episode, and not wanting to miss out, screamed for me to pick her up. How could I possibly resist the cries of my young daughter? As I walked down the hallway with Chloe still in my arms, heading toward the kitchen to greet Natalie, my nose was able to detect a particular odor I was now quite familiar with. Things were much worse than I feared, however; not only did Chloe need her diaper changed, but I noticed that there was some strange substance smeared on my shirt and quickly creeping down my trousers. The pleasure I felt holding Chloe in my arms quickly turned to one of "Oh, yuck!"

It's a Small World

Natalie had heard from friends that pregnancy and labor weren't particularly enjoyable, but some aspects of caring for a baby dampened her prospects for fun as well. She tells it like this:

There were so many things I used to take for granted before I had a baby. I enjoyed my job immensely, and although toward the later stages of my pregnancy I was ready to leave my place of employment, I missed sharing those spontaneous moments of fun with my colleagues.

Having a newborn baby also interrupted many of the things we used to do together as a couple. For example, we were not always able to finish a meal together, and there were many conversations that we just didn't get to finish; depending on their importance, we sometimes returned to where we left off hours later. As a mother I was busy meeting my baby's needs and often struggled to find the energy and time to recognize and respond to Glenn's needs. This meant that having fun was the last thing on my agenda—"I just want to be alone and sleep!" was arguably my most common catch cry. I wasn't focused on having fun; I just wanted to survive. I didn't have the creative energy to think about all of the things I would enjoy doing with Glenn; I was happy just to get out of the house!

> I felt as though my world had suddenly shrunk and that nothing else existed or mattered outside of caring for a newborn baby.

I felt as though my world had suddenly shrunk and that nothing else existed or mattered outside of caring for a newborn baby.

Entire conversations with other moms, friends, and Glenn were consumed by baby-related subjects. Although my vocabulary had expanded to include phrases like "Is it sterilized?" "Have you checked the diaper?" "The baby's got gas." "Is the baby allowed to eat that?" and "Where's the dummy?" (and I didn't mean Glenn; I meant the pacifier), it had also shriveled because I didn't have the same opportunities to engage in adult conversations of a meaningful, intelligent, nonbaby nature.

Another reason I struggled to have fun was that Glenn's work often involved breakfasts, lunch appointments, and dinner engagements with clients. So while I was feeling trapped at home,

I began to resent the fact that Glenn was able to get out of the house and enjoy meeting people. He could have nice meals in a relatively quiet place (at least assured of no interruptions by crying babies) and basically have a life that didn't revolve only around our newborn son—and I couldn't enjoy these activities with him. Sure, there were some bright moments like when we were able to relax and enjoy each other's company, spending a Saturday morning at the botanical gardens while Ben was on his best behavior, but having fun took so much more effort—and it was inextricably linked to whether Ben was demanding our constant attention.

Laugh It Off

Because we were tired or still coming to terms with some of the emotional adjustments a baby creates, even those normally lighter moments didn't result in spontaneous laughter. To help us through this challenging time, we tried to find some things that would provide an emotional, physical, or spiritual lift.

One example that reintroduced us to fun was anticipating with great delight the development of baby photos. That sometimes meant paying a little extra to get them developed at a one-hour print shop. Naturally, we always asked for triple prints—one copy for us and one for both sets of parents. Natalie's mom was always insistent she didn't want to miss out on any photos—even the ones that were out of focus! But for Natalie and me, there was something special about watching other members of our family, our friends, and colleagues at work appreciate the photos of our baby boy.

The other thing we really enjoyed was taking him for a walk in the stroller down to the park or shops where people would often stop to appreciate him. Not only was it nice to get out of the house and talk to other adults, it was nice seeing how our son could bring pleasure to other people.

Help from Friends and Family

Asking friends and family to help out brought us relief at times. But it never seemed to be enough. A number of times Natalie's parents babysat Ben while we went out for dinner at a nearby restaurant. We took the mobile phone with us in case her parents ran into difficulty. Although we were grateful for the break and the night out, we found it difficult to relax, and it just didn't seem to compensate for being up three times a night for the previous week. Natalie explains her feelings about asking for too much help:

My parents were wonderful, but I didn't want to abuse their willingness to help. We were fortunate that they lived close by and were willing to come and help. We also realized that there were

limits and that it wasn't always fun for them if we went out and Ben screamed his lungs out until we got back. Neither did I want to abuse my relationships with friends. Most of our friends were also raising young children and in need of support themselves, so we didn't want to add to their pressure by asking them to babysit.

Another reason why I didn't seek a lot of help was that deep down I am quite independent. I aspire to be a mother who enjoys being with her children, not one who is constantly trying to off-load her kids to someone else to have a break. Much to Glenn's frustration, I occasionally got this out of balance.

Fortunately, as I listened to stories from other mothers, I discovered some interesting ways that parents of newborns have tried to cheer themselves up and cross from desperation to sanity.

One girl who used to work with me in the same hospital told me how she saved up a lot of her money while she was pregnant so that she could use it to pamper herself during the first year of her baby's life. One friend discovered aromatherapy—she ran a hot bath, put the baby to bed, lit the candles, and . . . well, the word *bliss* comes to mind!

Many times Glenn and I would look out our window and notice that small groups of mothers would be wheeling their babies in their strollers past our house, clearly using it as an opportunity to exercise and get out of the house. Some even managed to power-walk! Similarly, on different occasions while Glenn was taking Ben for a ride in the stroller, he would encounter other dads who were giving their wives a break, and endeavored to make the most of it by going down to the shops to run some errands.

Some of my friends went back to work part-time and employed nannies. Others would have a housecleaner come in once a week or every other week to give the house a good cleaning. We also had a housecleaner while I was pregnant with Ben. It provided some great relief, particularly during the final weeks leading up to the time Ben was born. I remember Glenn's mother suggesting that we keep the housecleaner even after arriving home with Ben from the hospital. At a time when you seem to be spending a lot of money getting ready to have a newborn at home, this may not be possible. We made the decision not to continue with the housecleaner.

Following the "Dad" Crowd

Some liken becoming a dad to a rite of passage when boys become men. Suddenly, as a parent of a newborn I gained entry to a rather exclusive club where other dads give you that knowing look. They don't have to express themselves verbally to let you know they understand what you are going through. I quickly discovered that there were a wide range of activities they did to have fun—though I'm not convinced they always had a positive impact on the couple's relationship. For example, telling your wife that you're going four-wheel driving for the weekend may not result in her saying, "What a lovely idea. Go and enjoy yourself." And sex, which used to be spontaneous and fun, seems as elusive as the holy grail and requires as much strategizing to pull off as a corporate takeover. And even then, the best of plans can be undone by an unexpected cry of a newborn.

One thing Natalie and I managed for awhile, was alternating the mornings when each of us could go for a walk or run before I had to leave for work. Another friend's brother-in-law, an avid cyclist, bought a wind trainer and rode in the house during the baby's nap. You may have your own ideas to add to this list of how fathers can have victory over the baby blues.

Some "Depressing" Thoughts

No one questions or doubts that you have been on a steep learning curve, and you could be excused for feeling overwhelmed. There is no other moment in life similar to the one you are experiencing right now. It is also a moment full of contrasting emotions and thoughts—it is enriching and exhausting; it reveals the miraculous and the mundane; it is enlightening and confusing; it ignites hope and gives rise to anxiety; in spite of having prepared yourself as much as possible, you feel as though you know so little; and whereas once you lived for your own dreams, you are now charged with the responsibility of nurturing another's.

We must, however, introduce a word of caution. While it is not unusual and is even expected for a mother to feel anxious, confused, fearful, overwhelmed, or even sad coming home with a newborn, extreme sadness and depression that prevent a mother from functioning normally on a day-to-day basis may indicate postpartum depression. Other symptoms include feeling irritable, overeating, not having any interest in your baby, being afraid of hurting either the baby or yourself, difficulty making decisions, not being able to sleep, and feeling sad or crying a lot. Postpartum depression can begin a few days or even months after giving birth.

It is important that you visit your doctor if these symptoms persist. Don't delay in getting help, as postpartum depression can be treated with medication and/or counseling.

It is no wonder that many are overwhelmed with a sense of awe and responsibility. For these reasons it is quite understandable that

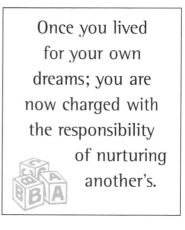

Once you lived for your own dreams; you are now charged with the responsibility of nurturing another's.

the intensity of these emotions together with the sheer hard work of caring for a newborn does not spill over into spontaneous laughter and fun.

Because this is a time of tremendous change, we encourage you to set aside some time to invest in some things you enjoy doing that are not necessarily baby-related. For Natalie it was a challenge to stop reading baby-care books every night and give herself permission to relax with a novel. Glenn liked to stay up late some nights to watch a good movie.

It is our hope that you will enjoy these challenges. Enjoying the journey might be hard at times, but it's not impossible! Have fun.

Quick Tips

- Plan and look forward to at least one thing you really enjoy doing that is not baby-related, such as maintaining a hobby or interest that you enjoyed before your baby arrived.
- Keep in contact with your friends so that you have a focus outside of your baby world as well as a link to some invaluable support (especially if they've traveled a similar path). Try to remember other people's anniversaries, birthdays, and special events with a phone call. Looking outward can help balance your perspective.
- If you're well enough, maintain physical activities like riding a bike or walking to elevate your mood.
- Hire a sitter or ask a relative to watch the baby so you can get away for at least two hours. (Yes, you may take the mobile phone.)

"Bright eyes cheer the heart;
good news strengthens the bones."[9]

Life Will Never
Be the Same

I remember it vividly as if it were only yesterday. In order to be prepared for the birth of our first baby (or at the very least, know a little about what to expect!), Natalie and I attended a series of maternity classes run at the hospital that we had chosen for the birth of our baby.

I think it was about the fourth session that my world was suddenly rocked when some of the words spoken by the maternity nurse registered with a thud. The maternity nurse had sensitively challenged any preconceived notions that we, as prospective parents, might have had about our lives being the same as they once were prior to having children. In the space of about three minutes, I realized that my relatively quiet and self-centered world was not going to be so peaceful any longer. Her words went something like this:

"If you normally look forward to weekends and Saturdays for rest . . . forget it! If you like to take a few hours to read the morning paper . . . forget it! If you like to take a leisurely stroll down the street to the bakery and pick up the papers . . . you'll be taking someone else along with you, and it may not be so leisurely, and it will more than likely be earlier than ever before. Breakfast in bed . . . forget it! In fact, it will take on a whole new meaning: You'll be willing to skip breakfast just to get a few extra precious minutes in bed. Your life will never be the same again!"

> **Saturdays took on a whole new meaning. Instead of going for a leisurely walk or taking my time reading the morning paper, there were new priorities.**

I imagined the nurse's words were supposed to have an effect similar to those of an army drill sergeant trying to instill the "fear of God" into his new recruits on their first day. Naturally, we laughed it off. We knew she was joking, and that we would still have lots of spare time to read the paper on the weekend or go out for a cappuccino or hot chocolate. Most of us attending this particular session convinced ourselves that she was just preparing us for the worst-case scenario, and that there wasn't much chance it would happen like this for us.

But then the baby came, and I couldn't believe it—the nurse was right! Saturdays took on a whole new meaning. Instead of going for a leisurely walk or taking my time reading the morning paper, there were new priorities.

I love my space on the weekend. After working with people all week, I view weekends as a time when I don't have to think too much about what they need and can finally set my own agenda for all of the things I want to do. Yet now, Natalie expected me to chip in to help break the morning routine she had become accustomed to from Monday through Friday. It seemed that all of a sudden, her need for space and the ability to get out of the house overrode my need for weekend relaxation. Instead of reading the morning newspaper I found myself occupying my newborn son.

Searching for Sanity and the Daily News

Although the nurse in the maternity class told us not to worry about keeping a clean house due to the increased demands on our time, we didn't feel comfortable living in a war zone. The only problem was, we had to learn how to clean the house as quietly as we could so as not to disturb our son while he was sleeping. Just as we finished cleaning the house and thought we might have a few moments to ourselves, Ben would wake up!

It was around this time, coincidentally perhaps, that we decided to outsource the lawn mowing to a friend. I've got to be honest and say that I also had an expectation that this would increase the likelihood of getting some extra sleep or downtime on

Saturday afternoons. Unfortunately, I forgot to tell my friend not to mow during sleep times (either our baby's or ours!).

Yep . . . in those first few weeks we were either too busy or too tired to worry about another one of our favorite pastimes—the traditional reading of the morning newspaper. I've got to confess that I am one of those fanatics who has to read the postmortem of the football game played the previous night even if my team wasn't playing. Some may even say that I am a sports junkie—I want to know what I missed while I was sleeping. In a moment of weakness Natalie might even divulge to someone how frustrating it was for her that I was great in remembering sports scores (in some cases, even from years earlier) yet still struggle with the home budget! Fortunately for me she doesn't have too many of those moments. In spite of having for years religiously read the Saturday morning papers to get all of the vital statistics, tradition accounted for little!

The maternity nurse was right; my life had changed. I now wondered how long it would be before I could once again read the Saturday morning newspaper on the morning it was printed. Only time would tell.

Counting My Losses

Apart from missing the "cappuccino" lifestyle we used to enjoy before having a baby, I found myself grieving a part of my life that had either ended or significantly changed. I know that grief is commonly thought of only in terms of how people feel if they have lost someone close to them. For me as a new mother, I felt as though there were some important things in my life that I had lost.

I know it must seem strange to talk about grieving at a time in my life when I had been looking forward to starting a family, but just because new things replace old things doesn't mean you can't miss those old things.

There were moments when tiredness from the constancy of caring for a newborn led to self-doubts that sometimes caused me to think of things that once were, and how life had changed. For me this included missing my work as an occupational therapist and the enormous satisfaction I enjoyed from it. I was grateful to hear from the families of my patients about how I had given them hope or made a difference. I appreciated being affirmed for the tasks I completed and how well I did them. Recognition from those I worked with also helped me to feel good about myself. These were now gone.

> I also grieved my friends and the way my relationship with many of them had changed.

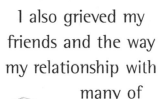

I also grieved my friends and the way my relationship with many of them had changed. Some I haven't seen since I went on maternity leave and our lives have taken different courses, while for others there hasn't been time or opportunity to catch up. It wasn't necessarily that my life had all of a sudden become busier; it was that it had become considerably different from the experiences of some of my friends. Common ground was crumbling away. However, in time I also discovered many new friendships from mothers' groups and playgroups that have become incredibly important to me.

I also grieved how my relationship with Glenn had changed. Yes, we were happy to be parents and were both very proud of our son, but we knew we didn't like some of the things we were seeing in each other. I know some would say that a crisis often brings out the worst in people and that to come through it they have to learn new things about themselves. While that was certainly true for us, it was more painful than what we wanted in a season when most of our energy was expended in adapting to the challenges of parenting. At times we simply didn't feel we had anything left to channel into our relationship. Our conflicts only increased the grief I felt at the loss of our relationship as it had once been.

Life Does Get Brighter

Whether or not you like to relax over a cappuccino, the point is your life has changed.

Although there are some who adjust well in the first few weeks after bringing a newborn baby home, even they on occasion experience self-doubt, tiredness, stress, frustration, anxiety, confusion, and grief. To use the old cliché, a new chapter in your life is being written and an old one has closed. You, however, might be able to embrace change better than others and have little problem in adjusting to the challenges of caring for a newborn and keeping your marriage relationship intact. Fantastic!

If on the other hand you happen to be similar to the many parents we have spoken to or interviewed when researching this book, then you know that you are in that zone where the shine might have worn off life and you are wondering when you are going to turn the corner and see things start to become a little brighter and easier. One important step you can take in preparing yourself to get through this zone is to acknowledge that self-doubts, conflicting emotions, and guilt are normal things for a parent of a newborn to experience, and they don't mean you don't love your baby. Remembering some of your favorite pastimes and wishing they were still a part of your life today does not make you a bad parent, and trying to find a babysitter while you go off to enjoy a cappuccino doesn't mean you are copping out.

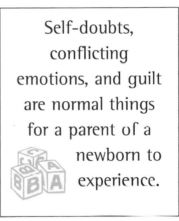

> Self-doubts, conflicting emotions, and guilt are normal things for a parent of a newborn to experience.

Quick Tips

- Share with each other how your weekends are different from what they used to be and what you miss about them. Explore how you might be able to help each other appreciate at least one thing on weekends that you used to do.

- Plan ahead for your free time, but don't overcrowd your schedule so that at the end of a weekend you feel exhausted, not refreshed. Plan one or two things, not three or four.
- Rather than remain in a constant place of grieving what you once had, embrace the season you are in, knowing that spring comes after every winter, no matter how dark. Recall with each other how you see your life changing and what you are looking forward to.

"A joyful heart
makes a face cheerful,
but a sad heart [produces]
a broken spirit."[10]

CHAPTER 12

What's a Cappuccino?

Although not quite on the same scale as a child anticipating lots of Christmas presents, I found myself looking forward to taking our baby down to the local café where I could enjoy a cup of coffee with Natalie. I mean, how hard could it be? What could possibly go wrong and interrupt our coffee experience? It didn't take me long to realize how naive I was.

We put our son into the stroller and walked the ten minutes to our local shopping area. *This is so easy!* we thought. Even before we made it to the coffee shop, our son fell asleep and we began to relax, thinking that we would finally have some quiet time together over an enjoyable cup of coffee. We didn't feel the need to place our order in a hurry, nor did we feel under pressure to gulp down our coffee and cheesecake, giving ourselves indigestion.

Little did we realize that we had allowed ourselves to be lulled into a false sense of security. Just as the order arrived at our table, our son woke up and decided to test his lung capacity. Not to worry—we had the pacifier, and instinctively popped it into his mouth. Ben promptly spat it out. Still no worry; we had toys. We dangled his favorite toy above his head, but that didn't work either. Finally, not wanting to be embarrassed any longer or be viewed as a menace to the peace-loving citizens trying to enjoy their coffee, we took him out of the stroller

> Now I began to understand what parents meant when they said if only they had their second baby first time around, things would have been considerably different!

and tried to console him. Having run out of options, Natalie took our son for a walk hoping that he would settle quickly. Sitting alone while I watched Natalie walk away and hearing Ben's cries diminish with every step was not really my idea of enjoying a cup of coffee.

The second time we attempted to relax over a cup of coffee, we enlisted the help of Natalie's parents. The original plan was for all of us to sit down and enjoy our coffee together. What actually happened was our son was handed around from one to the other until we had each finished our drink. Although the system worked reasonably well, it still wasn't my way of sitting relaxed in a café enjoying the coffee experience.

So was there a third time? Yes there was, but this time we didn't go out to a café. We stayed at home! We didn't have the stress of having to worry about the customers when Ben cried, and if our coffee was at risk of growing cold, we simply warmed it up in the microwave. Once again, not my idea of a pleasurable cup of coffee, but it worked. By the time our second son came along, we were rewarded with a mild-mannered baby who allowed us to go to the café, relax, and drink to our hearts' content! Now I began to understand what parents meant when they said if only they had their second baby first time around, things would have been considerably different!

What's in a Cup of Coffee?

Why are we placing such great importance on visiting a local café with your baby and enjoying a cup of coffee? Because it's activities like these that you used to enjoy that provided some enriching times for your relationship. This time together in an unhurried environment allowed you to discuss anything that took your fancy. You may also have considered moments shared like this as downtime or personal space where the both of you could wind down after a stressful week.

If you look forward to times of relaxation as a way to strengthen your relationship, you may need assistance in creating this time. Especially in the first few weeks, consider enlisting the help of baby's grandparents or other family members.

Quick Tips

- Work out what you think is the best time to discuss an issue together and ask your family or close friends to hold down the fort while you're on assignment.
- Try to maintain at least one thing that was important to you before your baby came along—for example, going for a walk or having friends over for dinner. It will remind you that not everything has been turned on its head.
- Those quiet, unhurried moments may seem a long way off and a thing of the distant past. If you miss going down to the local café for a cappuccino, arrange for some friends to go with you so they can take your baby for a walk while you relax and enjoy being together.

*"For then you will have a future,
and your hope will never fade."*[11]

CHAPTER 13

Not Tonight . . .
I'm Too Tired!

A favorite pastime of mine (Glenn) is walking into bookshops and looking at the various book titles in the self-help/health areas. One particular afternoon I found myself browsing in a bookshop after work. One book cover caught my attention with the word *SEX*. Below the caption was a cleverly crafted cartoon depicting a scene that most men can identify with—the amorous and hopeful look of a man in the mood for sex extinguished instantly by the woman's retort—"You've got to be joking!" I laughed and quickly placed the book back on the shelf before anybody else was able to see the connection.

Enough books have been written on the different emotional characteristics of men and women to send us to sleep. Nonetheless, emotional and physical intimacy is a part of our psychological makeup; woe to them who ignore it. I will never forget having a conversation with a man I had never met before while sitting on a plane flying to Brisbane. Somehow we got into a deep discussion about his marriage and how he had thought that having another baby would rejuvenate his relationship with his wife. He went on to tell me how he had become married to his work more than his wife, and that an overwhelming coldness had caused them both to become emotionally and physically distant. He thought that a baby would provide a common focus for their love and attention that would bring them closer together. Sadly, this didn't happen.

> My experience is that sex is far more satisfying to Natalie and me when we are on the same wavelength.

His work still demanded a lot of his time and energy, and by the time he arrived home from work, his wife was exhausted from caring for their newborn. She was also frustrated and angry, because at a time when she needed her husband to engage her and their newborn, he had not adjusted his life to meet the needs of another child and their barely surviving relationship.

Listening to this man describe his sad life immediately provided me with a wake-up call. All of the best self-talk and intentions weren't going to improve my relationship with Natalie. I knew that there were changes I needed to make in my life that would communicate to her how much she meant to me, and that my life with her and my children were far more important than responding to the demands of my work. I didn't find this easy, however. At times I felt trapped by the competing demands of work and family, and I regretfully admit, work often won the day.

"Perfect" Sex

One of the dangers of writing about intimacy and sex is the tendency to compare your own experience with that of other people. There have been a few times when I have read a magazine article or a book on how to improve my marriage—usually about someone's amazing sex life against the backdrop of a faultless life—and found myself falling short of their mark. We can make all the jokes we like about sex, such as "practice makes perfect" and "men want it most of the time, and women only some of the time," but what Natalie and I have discovered is that sex is hard work! Sure, sex is fun and pleasurable, it can be spontaneous or planned, and it can be the perfect finish to a day. So why is sex hard work? Because there are so many variables that can either contribute to its enjoyment or detract from it. It is more than just a physical act between two people; it is emotional, spiritual, and physical connection.

While I don't particularly subscribe to the theory that men crave only physical intimacy and women crave only emotional intimacy, my experience is that sex is far more satisfying to Natalie and me when we are on the same wavelength—we have taken the time to understand each other's needs, dreams, and desires. We have tried to ease each other's burdens and have engaged each other's world. We have listened to each other!

Unfortunately, this was a lot more difficult once our children were born, especially after our first child. There were times that Natalie was so uninterested in the sexual side of our relationship that I wondered if she would ever become interested again. I found myself falling into a destructive cycle that selfishly eroded the strength of our relationship. I thought, *If Natalie can't be bothered making the effort in an area that is important to me, then why should I try so hard in meeting her needs in other areas?* Honestly, I don't think we did a great job cultivating an enriching sex life at a time when fatigue, stress, and anxiety were present as constant enemies. Although we are now past those challenging days of caring for a newborn and have three young children, we still find ourselves working to protect our sexual relationship from those same things that can destroy intimacy and romance.

Sex: The Last Thing on my Mind

I have always found intimacy, sex, and romance some of the most difficult areas in our relationship. I understand that they are very important, but I came from a family that didn't always find it easy to be openly affectionate and affirming. While I certainly don't blame my parents for this, I have discovered that it takes a lot of effort to change something that has been a significant part of my makeup since I was a young child.

After having a baby, being intimate with Glenn was even harder for me. I have always been someone who likes to have my own personal space, and I found it really hard to cope with having a baby around me twenty-four hours a day. I felt like I was constantly on call, and there were times when Glenn couldn't help when I needed him to. By the time evening came around, I was looking forward to some space both emotionally and physically. So you guessed it—the last thing I felt like was sharing my soul or having sex.

At this time I also felt that my body was out of control. I had a big, flabby stomach, my breasts were sore from feeding, and I craved some physical space away from my baby. My hormones caused my emotions to fluctuate, and for the first couple of weeks in the afternoon all I wanted to do was cry. This just made me feel worse. Being unhappy with my appearance, feeling exhausted and sore, and being frustrated when Glenn didn't live up to my expectations all worked against our attempts to maintain and develop a healthy relationship—physically and emotionally.

Fatigue and fluctuating emotions certainly had a negative effect on our sex life and being intimate with each other. I began to feel as though I was a failure in this area of my life as well, not only in motherhood. I didn't have a whole lot of energy to focus on Glenn's needs or our needs as a couple. Nearly always it was the baby's needs that won out.

Use It or Lose It!

This created a problem I had not expected. When our home life began to return to some form of manageability and semblance of normality, I still found it hard to physically and emotionally connect with Glenn. A widening chasm had developed in our relationship during the early weeks of adjusting to a newborn, and we now needed to build a bridge back across it to restore intimacy. This meant we both had to work hard at our relationship. Because I felt my needs were not being met, my attitude soured. I'd think, *Why should I have to worry about meeting Glenn's needs when I'm so drained?* Although I knew at the time this was not a very mature way of thinking and I did not want to excuse my behavior, it did reflect how much I was struggling and how low my energy was.

> A widening chasm had developed in our relationship during the early weeks of adjusting to a newborn, and we now needed to build a bridge back across it.

One of my friends reminded me that the principle of "If you do not use something you lose it" applies to sex as well. As much as sex is wonderful and fun, I found that I had allowed many things to work against us in creating the necessary environment to enjoy being intimate with each other. Ultimately, I had to think about how to "get my groove back."

What do I mean by that? For me it was about doing some things that helped me to feel good about myself and gave me the energy and space I needed so I could begin focusing on what my relationship with Glenn needed. At times this meant spoiling myself—buying something nice for myself rather than my baby. As my mother said to me, "Your kids look great. You don't. Pamper yourself. You are worth it."

As a mother, I found it difficult to maintain intimacy in our relationship when I had nothing to give. It helped our relationship when I took the time to explain to Glenn that I needed to have some time away from our baby, even if it was just to take a nice bath or go to the gym. I know that it is hard to rebalance schedules when the baby comes, but it was important to regularly do something for myself.

> Merely hoping that things will return to normal after a few weeks of caring for a newborn is naive and wishful thinking. We did not imagine that a baby would affect our energy levels, communication, and sex life the way it did.

Affirm and Encourage Each Other

Talk about your needs as a couple and then try to work out a plan to address them. Merely hoping that things will return to normal after a few weeks of caring for a newborn is naive and wishful thinking. We did not imagine that a baby would affect our energy levels, communication, and sex life the way it did. Being unprepared for these challenges meant that we struggled for some time to recover from the damage they caused to our relationship. We had to swallow our pride and not wait for each other to initiate words of affirmation and encouragement or acts of service that

would give each other a little break and some needed space. By the time our second and then third child came along, we were a little wiser, but we still learned that we had to be careful not to take all the things we enjoy about our relationship with our sweetheart for granted.

Quick Tips

- Identify those things that may be driving a wedge between you and your spouse and destroying opportunities to be intimate.
- Recognize that intimacy is about more than just the enjoyment of sex and is as much about listening to each other and working together as a team.
- Choose an appropriate time and place to discuss how you feel about your relationship and what needs the both of you have. Be careful to listen without interrupting or getting defensive.
- Make an effort to speak affirming, loving words to each other. The right words spoken at the right time can

heal many wounds and defuse potentially energy-sapping arguments.

- One of our friends arranged for a babysitter to look after their infant for a few hours while they went off to a hotel for an uninterrupted coffee, bath, and . . . (you know the rest of the story).

"Never let loyalty and faithfulness leave you."[12]

CHAPTER 14

Seize the Day

By now, we'd discovered that our lives would never be the same as they once were, and "normal" had been redefined.

Just as the telephone and Internet revolutionized communications and two world wars during the twentieth century shaped the course of our history, so the arrival of our son influenced almost every single decision we were to make. He also challenged the boundaries of our relationship and gave us fresh insights into human nature as well as the power and vulnerability of love. We had many things to learn, and as a result, our lives would be stretched to new limits and enriched.

Glenn experienced those stretching experiences in this way:

There were many moments when I found myself wishing the day would finish so tomorrow could come. I gained strength from the hope that tomorrow might be better than the tiring present. Though in some cases the future was an improvement, I wasn't able to fully appreciate this stage of life. Many special moments slipped through my grasp because I couldn't find joy in the "now." Deep down, I knew I was missing out on the extraordinary experience of being a dad and learning many new things about myself, my relationship with Natalie, and my baby. Unfortunately, the sleepless nights put my mind and body into overdrive where they would merely do what was necessary to survive till the next day.

> Many special moments slipped through my grasp because I couldn't find joy in the "now."

At first I thought it was just a phase that would pass; however, the days rolled into the nights and there was no relief. I got frustrated with myself, with Natalie, and with Ben when I heard other people's stories about how their babies were a dream and slept through the night only days after coming home from the hospital. What was I doing wrong? Was Natalie doing something wrong? Was there something wrong with our son? Although I didn't realize it at the time, my frustration was causing me to question Natalie's decisions about how frequently she fed our son or attended to his needs. Naturally, this erosion of trust and confidence hurt Natalie and sabotaged our transition. It also reinforced the uncertainties and self-doubts she was beginning to have.

A New Mind-set

In spite of being born an *optimist,* according to my family and friends, I found myself struggling with a negative mind-set. When I reflect upon this period of my life, I realize that other life events colored my perspective.

On the one hand I was a dad; on the other I was grieving the loss of my mother whose health was deteriorating every day. I grieved the fact that Ben would not know her as I had—her warm, affectionate, fun-loving presence. I found it difficult for these emotions not to become entangled in the joy I felt being a dad.

The joys of being a dad, cradling my son for hours in my arms as he either slept or lay awake, singing to him as I bathed him, and watching him as he lay asleep in his crib were moments I will always remember. I appreciated the joy he brought to Natalie as she tucked him into her almost as if they were part of each other and nothing could separate them. I enjoyed watching how Ben became the center of attention whenever someone visited our home or when others would stop us while we were out walking so they could admire him. I'm not just talking about a handful of moments, but hundreds of them.

I often had to remind myself that my mother, who always had such a positive outlook on life, would not have wanted me to miss out on what new things today would bring. I know she would not have wanted me to focus on her absence, but instead to enjoy Ben and love him now, knowing that there would never be another today.

Hope for Tomorrow and Today

I struggled tremendously with how Glenn was feeling. He usually had lots of energy and could put a positive spin on most things no matter how negative they might appear, but I didn't have enough energy to help him in the way he probably needed. I had no doubt in my mind that this time for Glenn and our son, and for us as a family, would have been quite different if it had not coincided with his mother's terminal illness.

On a practical level, I had to change the focus of my life from my relationship with Glenn to the needs of our son. To an extent, our needs became quite secondary to those of caring for our newborn baby. It wasn't that we weren't important, but that our needs could wait and our baby's needs could not. Baby was always first! This was definitely the biggest adjustment we had to make.

Like Glenn, but for different reasons, I couldn't wait until some days had finished, hoping that tomorrow would be better. In the back of my mind there was always the hope that with each passing day, my skills as a mother would improve and that I would have less reason to be anxious, making rest and sleep more of a possibility. Although I wasn't wishing my days away, I was looking forward to each day being a little easier than the previous one.

One of the most powerful coping mechanisms people use to survive the circumstances they find themselves in is that of holding on to hope. Hope is that light at the end of the tunnel that is constantly becoming brighter and brighter as you get closer to it.

As a parent of a newborn, it is OK to look forward to things becoming a little easier (and they will!). The key is not to allow that hope to dominate your life to the extent that you miss out on some of the unique and wonderful moments you can share with your baby and your spouse during this time.

Remember the saying "You don't realize what you've got until you've lost it"? Before you know it, your baby will be a few months or even a few years old, and you'll wish that some things had not changed.

There may be times when you want your old life back and wish that your relationship with your husband or wife did not have to endure the things that it has, but together you have grown. The challenge of caring for your newborn 24/7 is greater than you had ever imagined, and you wonder if you'll ever experience the bliss of silence and space again. And yet, as the days roll into months and then years, you enjoy and become amazed by the glimpses of each other you catch in your child's smile, the sparkling eyes, the cheeky look, the antics, the way he talks, and his developing personality. How quickly he grows. First he's wrapping his tiny hand around your little finger, then he's taking your hand as you walk with him. All too soon, you're reluctantly letting go of his hand on the first day of school. Once reliant on you for survival, your child soon presents you with new challenges as he pushes the boundaries toward independence and you wonder, *How did he grow up so quickly?*

Seize today, for you hold the power to create something beautiful for tomorrow. Not only special memories you will treasure and one day recount to your grandchildren, but children who as adults will be unique in many ways and yet a reflection of you.

Yes, life will never be the same again, and rarely will there be a moment when you wish that it were!

Quick Tips

- You've reached the end of a tiring day. Reflect briefly on some of the moments you enjoyed, and share with each other how they made you feel.
- Be careful not to fall into the trap of comparing your situation to that of others. Each situation is different and every newborn unique.
- Take stock of your attitude. Discuss some practical ways you can support each other, as your needs may have changed in recent weeks.
- Rather than focus on those things you have found difficult to adjust to, discuss with your spouse how your baby is blessing your life.

"There is profit in all hard work."[13]

Notes

1. Proverbs 24:3-4
2. Proverbs 2:11
3. Proverbs 6:6, 8
4. Proverbs 12:18
5. Proverbs 10:12b
6. Proverbs 11:25b NIV
7. Proverbs 1:5 NIV
8. Proverbs 14:29
9. Proverbs 15:30
10. Proverbs 15:13
11. Proverbs 23:18
12. Proverbs 3:3a
13. Proverbs 14:23a